Jacob has written a masterpiece that will completely shift your entire paradigm as he opens a door to a whole new world of living in the supernatural, heaven, interacting with angels and amazing encounters with God that most people only read in the Bible or history books. Jacob is now opening this world of wonder to you and giving you the keys to living heaven on earth literally. May God totally shake and transform your life as you dare to read what God really has in store for you!

Dr. David Herzog
David Herzog Ministries
Sedona, AZ

In these last days, God is releasing supernatural power in many ways: healings, miracles, angelic encounters, transportations, translations and the knowledge of future events to his people. In *Encountered*, Jacob Biswell, shares some of his experiences in all these dimensions so that you can prepare yourself for all God wants for you. I hope that his testimony will motivate you to seek God and trust Him in the supernatural life you are called to experience.

Joan Hunter
Joan Hunter Ministries
Tomball, TX

Jacob is a spiritual son of mine who I met when I prophesied over him about his marriage. We have walked together from that time. As a board member of their ministry I have watched as they have sought counsel with humility and desire to follow hard after Yahweh. In this book, Jacob takes the reader down the path of his own experience and then blankets it with the word of Jehovah. This will help the reader be encouraged in their own experiences and teach them the correlation between encounters in scripture and encounters of our own.

Dr. Candi MacAlpine

Apostle/Prophet with CIAN under Dr. Bill Hamon

Founder Destiny Training Center, Oakhurst, California

As a pastor and director of a House of Prayer, the ability to read a book to completion in a single sitting is a rare joy in my life. I was ecstatic that I finished *Encountered* in one morning! Each chapter drew me into the depths of Jacob's personal yet succinct stories of the stunning activity of the Lord in his life. In humility Jacob also shares his journey of maturing in response to his experiences and revelation of submission to accountability that give needed clarity to current prophetic culture. Expect something new and provoking when you read his book!

Cynthia Griffith

Director College Station House of Prayer

College Station, TX

After reading the book, I recalled the period of time in which he speaks about his encounter with "The Flaming Sword." God had revealed to several intercessors to intercede for him and call for the deliverance from the darkness he was in. We never knew the extent of his involvement until reading the book. The spiritual world is real. Satan wants our children, especially when they have accepted Jesus early in life. I found this very enlightening as to the struggles many are drawn into because of the desire for the supernatural.

Rev. Birdella A. Tucker

Pearl Box Ministries

Reedley, CA

ENCOUNTERED

JACOB BISWELL

One man's journey of
visitations, open heavens
and encounters which can
only be described as
supernatural.

ENCOUNTERED

Expanded Edition

ENCOUNTERED
BY JACOB BISWELL

Production assistance provided by LifeWiseBooks.com

Interior Layout and Design | Yvonne Parks | PearCreative.ca

ISBN-13: 978-0692463642
ISBN-10: 069246364X

DEDICATION

To my first love, Jesus. All glory belongs to you! This book wouldn't exist if you hadn't shown up. You changed my life when I first met you at six years old, and you have been wrecking it in the best way imaginable ever since. May I always keep your fiery gaze at the front of my mind.

TABLE OF CONTENTS

FOREWORD

Elisha gives us an amazing insight into both how a genuine prophet functions and how he or she brings significant changes to environments and atmospheres. Elisha's servant, panicked by the sight of the surroundings, reports back in fear. Here is Elisha's response:

> *(17) Then Elisha prayed and said, "O LORD, I pray, open his eyes that he may see." And the LORD opened the servant's eyes and he saw; and behold, the mountain was full of horses and chariots of fire all around Elisha.*
> *(18) When they came down to him, Elisha prayed to the LORD and said, "Strike this people with blindness, I pray." So He struck them with blindness according to the word of Elisha.*
> *(19) Then Elisha said to them, "This is not the way, nor is this the city; follow me and I will bring you to the man whom you seek." And he brought them to Samaria.*
> *(20) When they had come into Samaria, Elisha said, "O LORD, open the eyes of these men, that they may see." So the LORD opened their eyes and they saw; and behold, they were in the midst of Samaria.*[1]

We find three significant and very applicable points for the genuine function of prophets today:

1. Elisha's obvious capacity to see and understand what was happening in the realm of the Spirit.
2. His ability to access that realm and even shift others (in this case his servant) into that realm.
3. Of most importance, his ability to deal with the opposition and create massive change to the situation

resulted in release and freedom. I refer to this as bringing "governmental shifts."

Elisha's governmental and spiritual authority in the Spirit realm, which affected the natural realm, is a demonstration of the true and proper function of what we now look to for a New Testament Prophet; one who can literally "see" rather than say they see (when in fact they are simply perceiving). They create such a governmental shift in the Spirit as well as the natural realm that from the moment they arrive to a ministry appointment, everything for that church, ministry, and environment is forever shifted, brought into greater freedom, and propelled into the next phase of God's purposes. The church today is in desperate need of genuine prophets with such capacity and grace on their lives. It has been my privilege to witness first-hand the rising up and development of one such prophet: Prophet Jacob Biswell.

I have witnessed first-hand Prophet Jacob functioning as a true, genuine, and authentic modern-day prophet. He is brilliantly accurate in his Gift of Prophecy and amazingly graced to create governmental shifts to the environment where he is ministering. Miracles are clearly evident when he prays for people for healing, operating without hype but with genuine love and compassion. His preaching touches the heart of current issues facing the congregation he is ministering to and the long-term fruit is testified of long after he is gone. This book, *Encountered,* details a journey and experience of the development of a true prophet of God. But of greatest importance, this book demonstrates the function of what a true New Testament Prophet looks like.

Personally, I am very concerned as to the watering down of the ministry of a prophet that has occurred during my tenure as a Prophet (over 30 years and recognised as such independently of myself). People who are self-proclaimed prophets and people with a finely tuned Gift of Prophecy are falsely recognised as Prophets. They are unable to create the level of governmental shifts that are required for the church today. Indeed, people are blessed by their ministry, but do they prove their gifting by forever creating a mark in the ground that people would say "When that prophet came to us, everything changed for the better!"

I believe this book, *Encountered*, brings both direction and great encouragement to the fact that God is indeed raising up a new breed of prophets exhibiting the signs and wonders necessary for our world today. Prophet Jacob is one such prophet, and this book will bring enormous hope and encouragement to all those who look for a greater glory.

BRENT DOUGLAS
Senior Pastor, Encounter Christian Centre
Auckland, NZ
www.encounter.org.nz

ENDNOTES

1. 2 Kings 6:17-20 (NASB)

ACKNOWLEDGEMENTS

To my wife Anna, you have stuck by my side through some of the craziest trials I have ever been through. You have been my rock, my cheerleader, my confidant, my best friend. Thank you for being steadfast and keeping me grounded. I love you!

To Birdella Tucker and Mary Renteria–you taught me to pray, to receive, to prophesy, and to hear. Words cannot express my gratitude.

To Jill Austin, your life was an example of what it means to live a lifestyle of visitation. Thank you for mothering me and I know you are having a blast living every day in His presence. I will see you in glory some day!

INTRODUCTION

One Encounter with the Lord can change everything! It is my life's mission to spread the message of amazing Love that encountered me at a young age. I was a peculiar child. I "knew" things others didn't. I saw things few would mention.

I remember walking down the aisle to the altar at four or maybe five years old to give my life to Jesus. It was a decision that would lead me on a lifelong adventure. That adventure has birthed what you hold in your hands—just a taste of the opportunity that sits before any person desiring a relationship with the one who loves like no other.

"Mommy, the president is going to do something bad with a woman and the whole world will know." I can still see the image of the president on the TV in my dream. He was denying that he had done anything wrong, but I knew that he had. I woke up in a panic and rushed to tell my mom. I can still remember the look on my mom's face when I told her what I had dreamt. This was 1996.

This was a common occurrence in my house as a child. I would dream something, tell my mom, and then it would come to pass. This time, my mom just couldn't believe what I was saying. She said, "Oh honey, I think you had a nightmare." I refused to agree.

Fast forward two years to December 1998. I am sitting in the living room watching as the man in my dream says he didn't do what he was being accused of. I looked at my mom and said, "He's lying. I knew this was going to happen. God showed me." My mom apologized profusely for not believing me.

I have had people say to me, "So are you psychic?" My answer is always, "No, I just know who my Father is." This is the reality of those who are in the Kingdom of God, and it is accessible to anyone who will press into knowing the Father.

I believe there are many who will read this and say, "I've had those same things happen to me. Are you sure I'm not a psychic?" Yes. I am sure. However, without Jesus, your gifting will remain unredeemed and will stay in a soulish realm. The best way to steward your gifting and actually become more accurate is to get in relationship with the one who sees all, knows all and hears all.

The purpose of this book is two-fold. First, it is a compilation of multiple encounters. I originally wrote this book much shorter with less detail, and over time discovered that there was much more I could share to help the body of Christ and those seeking something more.

Secondly, it is to equip you for the encounters that God has awaiting you in what can be termed as "the last days." It has been the cry of my heart to see a proper balance brought to the body of Christ in the realm of the supernatural. More than a cry, I believe it is my mandate to raise up a generation of believers that know the manifest presence of the Lord and can discern light from darkness. At the end of every encounter, I will share wisdom and revelation that I have gained. It is my heart to release biblical revelation so that you, too, can encounter the Lord in this way.

My heart is simply to encourage you with my life–that I may be a living Epistle.[1] Each encounter brought a different lesson that is applicable to every believer.

Across the earth today, there are people who understand what it is to encounter the supernatural; to see the unseen realm. Sadly, this group is a small fraction of the church. While some in the body of Christ have encountered such things, the reality of such a potent mix of these radical believers is in small amounts.

As you read this personal account of my journey within these pages, I pray that you will receive an impartation of what the Lord has given to me. The Bible says the testimony of Jesus is the spirit of prophecy, so you can have what I have. As we go on this journey together may you find yourself encountering the realm of the supernatural and, in essence, become naturally supernatural. May you find yourself with greater knowledge of what He has promised the believer in the Word.

May His presence encounter you as He has **encountered** me.

Jacob Biswell

ENDNOTES

1. 2 Corinthians 3:2

"And he turned him unto his disciples, and said privately, blessed are the eyes which see the things that ye see: For I tell you, that many prophets and kings have desired to see those things which ye see, and have not seen them; and to hear those things which ye hear, and have not heard them."

LUKE 10:23-24

CHAPTER ONE

THE PERSON OF JESUS

June 1996

"And as he journeyed, he came near Damascus: and suddenly
there shined round about him a light from heaven..." [1]

I remember the very moment He stepped into the room. The air became pure and clean with His presence. The hair on the back of my neck stood on end. My six-year-old body began to tremble as I knew I was no longer alone. Awakened from my sleep, I knew someone was standing in the room.

This wasn't new for me. As far back as I could remember, I could "see." This "seeing," however, had not been a gift, or at least it wasn't in my mind. I had been tormented by the demonic. I could see the evil spirits, and they made sure I knew they were there. This time, however, was different. Fear was nowhere to be found. My heart fluttered with excitement this time. I was nervous about opening my eyes, but when I did, I encountered the One who would change my life forever.

As I carefully opened my eyes, I was nearly blinded by the most radiant light I had ever seen or have ever seen to this day. It welcomed me into an embrace, a divine exchange. I still hadn't looked to see the source of light, but as I turned my head to see who or what was in my room, my breath seemed to escape me. I immediately knew who it was, and I couldn't believe that He was in my room. In all His beauty, there He was. The Person of Jesus. Love Himself! The very one who had captured my heart, the one I had decided to follow even at six years of age.

He was standing there in radiating glory, emitting the very essence of Heaven and illuminating the room with a light that was neither painful nor dim. Trembling, I sat up in my bed and stared straight into His eyes. Oh, His eyes! They emanated love! Not just the normal feel-good love, but what I would later come to understand as Liquid Love. This love was pure, unadulterated, and something that I had never, ever experienced before.

As I looked into His eyes, it was as though I was looking into a distant galaxy, a place never seen by the human eye. They were the most piercing blue eyes I have ever seen, and yet they weren't just blue. They were an array of colors; colors that have never been seen on the earth before. His eyes were like John described, a flame of fire.[2]

I don't know how else to describe the feeling of sitting before Him other than my six-year-old mind knew that love had hugged me tighter and held me closer than ever before, and yet He hadn't even reached the bedside. It was difficult to look away from his eyes, but I had noticed he was wearing the most brilliant, white robe. Around his shoulders was draped a brown head scarf. His hair was brown and shoulder-length with a full beard. He reached his hand out and there they were, the nail scars. It really was Him. Until this point, not a word had been exchanged between us. Then... He spoke.

"Jacob, you know who I am don't you?" His voice made my little body quake.

"Yes, you're Jesus," I replied. I had no framework or language for what I was experiencing and yet here He was in my bedroom in Dinuba, California. The King of the Universe was standing before me; the one whom I loved to tell people about! I loved Jesus so much! Never did I imagine that this Jesus, the one whom I loved would ever visit me. Yet here He was.

Our eyes were locked. I felt no fear or trepidation. I was looking into what I can only describe as "Home". I was home in His gaze; I was loved, accepted and I somehow understood that no matter what, all I had to do was remember His eyes and all the world would become calm.

As I gazed into the eyes of love, He spoke again, "Jacob, I have come to visit you to tell you how much you are loved and that no matter what happens, I am always right here for you. I love you Jacob and I have very big plans for your life. You will tell many people about the Father's love, but you must always remember how much He loves you."

As soon as He finished speaking, He brushed his hand across my face and embraced me. I can still feel His embrace today. With that, He smiled one more time, turned around, walked away and was gone. As quickly as He had come, He was now gone. I crawled back into bed and I remember lying there trying to process what had just happened. All I knew was how much love I had experienced. I will never forget what it felt like to be in the presence of Liquid Love. I don't remember falling asleep that night but I remember holding onto that moment so tight. Little did I know that it would be *that* moment that prepared me for the things that I would later experience. Even now as I write, I can feel that same feeling course through my body that I felt all those years ago. Those eyes still remain as clear as they were in 1996.

Over time, I would search for pictures of Jesus that resembled who I saw, but could never find anything close. It wasn't until 2008, over 12 years later, that I finally saw the face of Love accurately depicted. I was attending a school in Redding, California when I came across a portrait painted by a young girl named Akiane. When I saw her painting of Jesus, I instantly crumpled to the ground because it was who I saw a decade earlier. It was the same Jesus and what caught me was the depiction of his eyes. When I saw them I was instantly back in my childhood bed fixated on those eyes so alive with love; eyes that burned with Holiness.[1] Needless to say, I was overcome with emotion.

Since that time, I have heard others speak about encountering those eyes of love, the very person of Jesus. As a matter of fact, I have heard many stories of people being saved after an encounter with Jesus, especially in the Middle East; Muslims by the thousands are coming to know Jesus through encounters with Him.

My prayer is that you would encounter the eyes of Love. I pray that the person of Jesus would become so real to you. May His flaming eyes of Love be burned into your spirit so you find rest in them as I have.

TEACHING MOMENT:
THEOPHANY

I have often been asked, "Does Jesus really visit people? Didn't that stop with the Bible?"

I can't find a single chapter or verse in the Bible that says, Christ stopped visiting people.

It is never my intention to cause someone to think more highly of Jacob Biswell—my life's purpose is to point people to the person of Jesus. So, why did Jesus show up to me? I can't give you a blanket answer, but I can help you build faith for your own encounters.

John 14:21 says, "He that loveth me shall be loved of my Father, and I will love him and will manifest myself unto him."

I absolutely love this verse, specifically the word manifest. In the Greek, this word is emphanizō, which means to literally "appear, show one's self, or to come into view."[2] This is the same word that is used in Acts 10:40 when it says God raised him and showed him off publicly. It's also used when the angel manifested or appeared to Joseph in Matthew chapter one.

No figure in Scripture had as many encounters with God through theophany as Moses. The word theophany is defined as a, "Manifestation of God that is tangible to the human senses."[3]

God appeared to Moses in the fire of a burning bush[4] causing Moses to hide his face. At Mt. Sinai, Moses went up to the mountaintop to worship God. He saw God at a distance and was invited into God's presence, remaining there for 40 days. Later, Moses met "face to face" with God.[5]

There is so much scriptural precedence for encountering the Lord face to face. Understand, that this is your portion, too! Love the Lord, seek His face and He will manifest himself to you!

ENDNOTES

1. Revelation 1:14

2. Acts 9:3

3. "Emphanizō." *Smith's Bible Dictionary.* Barbour Publishing: 2012. *"The KJV New Testament Greek Lexicon."* http://www.biblestudytools.com/lexicons/greek/kjv/emphanizo.html. Accessed 31 July 2017.

4. Exodus 3:1-6

5. Exodus 33:11; Numbers 14:14; Deuteronomy 34:10

CHAPTER TWO

THE ANGEL OF COMFORT

November 1998

"For there stood by me this night the angel of God, whose I am, and whom I serve..." [1]

In November of 1998, my biological father passed away. It was sudden but not unexpected as he had been ill for quite some time. However, no eight-year-old anticipates the moment their daddy passes away. Needless to say, I was overcome with grief. I remember his funeral like yesterday; it was the day after Thanksgiving. I can still hear my eight-year-old voice saying to people that it was "alright" and that "he was with Jesus." I thought I needed to be strong, and yet on the inside I recognized my emotions. I remember specifically sitting on our pastor's wife's lap thinking that if I could run away and hide it would all be okay. When we arrived home that day, I spent my time sitting outside trying to have fun with my cousins, all the while dying on the inside.

I went to bed that night very distraught and finding no comfort, asking God to help me through the pain. For being but eight years old, I was very mature and had a pretty good grasp on my emotions. I remember falling asleep sometime during the night, crying. It was at some point during that night that I was awakened by a light tap on my shoulder. I looked up only to see one of the most beautiful faces I have ever seen. The contours of His face were perfect. His straight brown hair hung right at his shoulders and his skin was shimmering with glory. His smile was so beautiful!

He looked down at me, placed His hand on my face, and said, "Jacob, you don't have to worry or be afraid. God is going to be your Father from here on out."

I asked him, "What is your name?"

He replied, "I am Comfort."

And with that he was gone, leaving behind the smell of roses. I wept softly, no longer from sadness but from peace, knowing that even though I had lost my earthy father, I had a heavenly Father who cared for me and would always be there for me. I experienced the reality of *Shalom* that night. *Shalom* is the Hebrew word for peace and means nothing lacking, nothing wanting, nothing broken.

TEACHING MOMENT:
ANGELIC VISITATIONS

When dealing with the supernatural, particularly angels, some tend to be highly excitable and go overboard. Paul said they end up being deceived. They end up in a ditch on the side of the road because they did not bother to learn the instruction given in God's Word.

According to the Prophet Joel, supernatural manifestations will be more prominent in these last days.[2] Angels will come to direct, to change circumstances, to guide, to protect, and to provide for true Believers in Christ. Because of these increased manifestations, we need some basic guidelines to follow concerning all revelations, all visions, and all angelic appearances.

"But all these worketh that one and the selfsame Spirit, dividing to every man severally as he will."[3]

No one can wake up in the morning and decide, "Today I'm going to have a vision," or "Today I'm going to give someone a big prophecy." I have had several major visitations, manifestations, and appearances of angels. I have also had multiple visitations of the Lord Jesus Christ. Never once did I pray for any of these visitations or decide that I was going to step out into the supernatural. Any time I was caught up in a trance, had an open vision, or even a dream of guidance, revelation, or warning, I had nothing at all to do with it. God willed it, not me. I was simply minding my own business, cooperating with the will of God for my life, and the Holy Spirit moved unannounced.

Some people will have visions. Some people will not have visions. Having visions does not make you more spiritual than someone else. The Bible does not say, "Those who see angels are spiritually mature and have more faith." Only God can determine who will have these manifestations and why. It is a good thing, too, because some people are so extreme that if they did see an angel, they would try to catch him in a jar like a firefly. Angels are not for "catching." They are not genies in Aladdin's lamp. They come to change our circumstances, to give us direction, protect us, to cause provision to come to us and to deliver us. However, the manifestation of angels must be left to God's will alone.

There are approximately 300 references to angels in the Bible. One hundred and four of them are manifestations and visitations to men and women. Yet not one of those people was praying to see an angel when it occurred.

ANGELS DO NOT REPLACE THE HOLY SPIRIT

"But the Comforter, which is the Holy Ghost, whom the Father will send in my name, he shall teach you all things, and bring all things to your remembrance, whatsoever I have said unto you."[4]

Notice the Holy Spirit will teach you all things, not the angels of God. Some people think God sends angels to teach them, and they end up in a spiritual quagmire. The Holy Spirit alone is our teacher. The Bible says the angels of God desire to consider the things that God has revealed to us. It does not say angels come to reveal God's word to us.[5]

One of the biggest false religions in the world came about because of an angel "teaching" a man from Vermont foolish revelation that is not in the Bible. Of course, that was a false angel, but the man was so ignorant of the word of God he did not know the difference and built a world-religion based on Satan having deceived him.

"But when the Comforter is come, whom I will send unto you from the Father, even the Spirit of truth, which proceedeth from the Father, He shall testify of Me."[6]

The Bible says the Holy Spirit will always and only testify of

Jesus. In other words, He will only teach in line with God's Word and always give glory to Jesus.

A PRAYER FOR HEALING

I heard the Lord say to me, "I'm going to send the Comforter to those who have been grieving for years." That is my prayer for you. Some of you have been struggling with grief and you haven't been able to receive peace; this chapter is specifically for you!

Below is a prayer for you to pray. Experience the peace that the Comforter, the Holy Spirit, brings. You may still be grieving over a loss but receive comfort now. Shalom means Nothing lacking, nothing wanting, nothing broken.

"Father, today I release the pain I have held onto through the grieving process and I ask that you remove grief from my life. I receive the Shalom of Heaven and today I declare that I will no longer be stuck in the grave, but I will rise up in the life that You have provided. In Jesus' name, Amen!"

ENDNOTES

1. Acts 27:23
2. Joel 2:28-29
3. 1 Corinthians 12:11
4. John 14:26
5. 1 Peter 1:12
6. John 15:26

CHAPTER THREE
THE FLAMING SWORD

June 2004

*"And immediately the angel of the Lord smote him,
because he gave not God the glory..."* [1]

"Who maketh his angels spirits; his ministers a flaming fire..." [2]

My life in Christ has not all been wonderful, glory-filled years. I have
paid a price to walk at this level of encounter, and I have seen things I
wouldn't wish upon anyone. With that said, please know that some of
what I share in this chapter is simply because it happened and is in no
way meant to glorify the enemy whatsoever. I firmly believe the enemy is
a defeated foe, and I give no power to him at all.

In the summer of 2002, I found myself in a very strange spot. I was
reading the Bible regularly and finding myself rather dissatisfied with
"normal Christianity." The more I went to church, the more frustrated
I became. By this time, at 12 years of age, I was already preaching and

had even done some itinerant ministry. I knew the Word, and I had a relationship with God. However, what I was finding more often than not was that the traditional Pentecostal denomination I had grown up in had no grid for the supernatural beyond Acts 2—the baptism of the Holy Spirit. I was seeking power and not finding it in the church.

I was part of a service club. One evening a pastor in the group approached me and said, "You're searching, I can tell. I would love to invite you to a meeting where you can see real power." Of course, I was intrigued. How could I say no? If anyone could show me power, a pastor certainly could, right?! I was very excited, but little did I know this would send me into a near-death experience with a cloud of darkness that would last for the next two years.

I remember vividly the night he picked me up. I told my parents I would be going to a church meeting. I really had no clue where I was going, but I knew I was going to encounter the power for which I had been searching. We drove for what seemed like an eternity until we finally reached an old barn. There were several cars parked outside. It was quite dark out and I wasn't fully sure where we were. I knew we were at least 25 minutes from my home, but the car ride had left me so invigorated that my sense of direction was completely gone. It was so far gone that even if I had wanted to leave at that point I would have had no clue how to get home.

As we exited the car my "friend" said quietly, "Now don't say a word. They have already begun." Suddenly, I was very nervous. We walked around the back side of the barn to enter through a side door. There was not much light. In fact, the only light present was from flickering candles spread out across the room. My skin crawled as I looked to see if my angels were with me. I was comforted by the fact that I could see they were there. After my encounter with Jesus at age 6, I was able to see two angels that went with me wherever I am. I can either see or sense the presence of my guardian angels.

I gazed around the room at the circles of people all gazing at the center of the circle. It was then I realized where I was; I had entered a satanic coven. Yes, you are reading this correctly. A pastor, whom I knew through a service club and was widely accepted in the community had brought me to a satanic coven. What was even more shocking was that this man was the leader.

You would think I would have left immediately, but I was transfixed at the fact that there was actually power in the room. It was undeniably real. I watched and listened as they performed their rituals and chants. What really grabbed me was when people from the coven began to bring up those whom they invited to receive their "healing." One by one, they would approach this leader, who would "anoint" them with blood, and they would receive their healing. The enemy will always attempt to counterfeit the real deal. I would see things like this happen again and again over the next two years. It finally came to a point where it no longer impressed me; it simply became common place.

There is so much more I could share about what I saw, and perhaps one day I will. But for now, please understand that I am simply laying a foundation. This is just the tip of the iceberg, but I share this to help you understand the impact of the encounter that I will share toward the end of the chapter.

As I said, the darkness stayed in my life for two solid years. I couldn't pull out, and I tried in the beginning, but every time it would suck me right back in. For two years, I entertained darkness. I would attend church semi-regularly; I was part of an intercessors' group from time to time, but I never missed a Saturday night with the "group." The pastor picked me up at the same time every week, and off to the barn we would go, my parents none-the-wiser.

Fast forward to June 2004. There was one Saturday night that my normally happy-go-lucky pastor friend picked me up, but this night he was in a very different mood. He didn't speak to me the entire car ride as we sped through country roads. As we pulled up to the normal meeting spot, he nearly shouted at me with an expletive, "Don't say a '*blank*' word, don't even look when he comes in!" I thought to myself, "Who is 'he'?" We entered the barn as usual, but this time there was only one light to be seen. I stood in my usual spot on the outer circle. There was an eerie hush in the room as everyone stood faces down.

Somewhere behind me, I heard movement. I did not dare turn my head. I needed no introduction as the hair on the back of my head stood on end. I was frozen in fear. If it hadn't been for the fact that my guardian angels were with me, I don't know what I would've done. Even so, I knew who this was—it was the old dragon himself. For some reason, he chose this little gathering outside a rural farming community to make his entrance.

He walked right past me, almost touching shoulders, but I did not look at him. I could sense his eyes on me. He took those in the inner circle through the door towards the front of the barn, a place I had never been before. I stood in place, and for the first time in nearly two years I began to pray in the Spirit. I'm not sure why I did this, but for 45 minutes I stood there praying silently under my breath. Finally, the one who had gotten me into all of this emerged from that room and came straight towards me. Angrily he snarled, "Let's go!"

He drove me home that night, not saying a word. I didn't know it would be the last time I would ever see him. I was confused as to what had happened, but I knew I must have interrupted something with my praying.

That week was the strangest. I longed to go back in that room of power, even though I knew it was pure evil. I had constant thoughts about it. Soon, however, I would lose all desire to ever go back. As the week dragged on, I looked forward to Saturday night. On Friday night as I was sleeping in my room, I was suddenly awakened by someone calling my name. This was not something new to me, it had been happening for years, whether angelic or demonic. This time, however, seemed different. There was an entirely different atmosphere in the room. As I sat up to see who was there, I was immediately aware of the being in my room. This was indeed a heavenly messenger.

Standing before me was a very large angel with a flaming sword. I wasn't afraid of him. As a matter of fact, I scoffed as I asked, "Who are you?" I had developed quite the antipathy for the angelic, even though I credited my life to their presence. It's amazing how much pride will blind you to reality.

He spoke, firmly but quietly, "Jacob, I am sent by the Father for your repentance. Jacob, you must repent."

I laughed, "Ha! I will do no such thing…" and in my prideful arrogance I reached for his sword. It burned as it sliced my middle finger. I still bear the mark of this encounter.

He looked at me with such intensity and said, "Jacob, the Lord has sent me to collect you. If you don't change now, He will take your life. You will lose your soul, and it is not His will for you to perish."

As I sat there thinking, for the first time in ages, I felt conviction prick my heart. My heart began to melt before the Lord. I wept and cried out to God, "Father, please forgive me for ever running from you to find another source. I must know you! I will follow you all the days of my life, but I must see your work on the earth! I must see your power in greater measure than I ever saw with the enemy!"

The angel reached down and touched my head. He said, "Jacob, know that from this day forward, the mark of God is upon you. You are sealed in His love, and you will see His handiwork before your eyes."

I don't remember what happened next, but I do remember lying in my bed, weeping for hours until I was finally awakened by the sound of the lawnmower out back. I got up that Saturday morning knowing my life had been drastically changed. I never did see my "friend" again. I later found out that he had resigned, packed up his family, and left that very same weekend.

After encountering the angel in my bedroom, I would go on to see some incredible miracles birthed in the raw power of God. In the next chapter, you will read about one of these miracles that truly showed the reality of God in my life. I want to take the time however, to share with those who may have come out of a background like this or may even still be in it.

There really is a better way—His name is Jesus. The reality I have come to understand is that lucifer or satan really has no power. He is a defeated foe, a fallen creation, and the only true power comes through Jesus Christ.

I know this seems strange to hear that the one you're serving and have promised your life to has no power, but it's true. He's defeated and is not equal to God. I encourage you to reach out to me, I have included my contact information at the back of the book. Please write to me. I would love to minister to you. But most of all, know that Jesus really does love you, and if you choose to swear allegiance to Him, your life will never be the same.

TEACHING MOMENT:
THE JOURNEY OF DELIVERANCE

I must, for the sake of clarity, take time to explain my journey after the coven. The encounter I had was just the beginning of a journey to total freedom from darkness. You see, anytime we stray from the true source, which is Christ, we position ourselves in a very dangerous place.

By opening myself to the demonic powers, I allowed my soulish realm to be polluted. One of the many misconceptions in the church is that Christians cannot have demonic influence. This is a tragedy —one that sadly affected my journey.

Even though I'd renounced all of the activity, I needed deliverance. Thankfully, a sweet intercessor recognized this several years later and initiated a 5-year journey of complete freedom.

While the encounters I share in this book are pure, there was a period of time I would go in and out of encounters against my will. I would be sitting at a table and fall out into a trance, or I would be with a group of people and be gone again. It got to the point where I would never know if I was in or out of one. My wife was quite upset, and it became really difficult to do everyday life. I would be gone, and my body would be taken over by what we thought was the Holy Spirit. The key became very clear; we all have a will. When these encounters began to take place, I began to give up my free-will. I was under the influence of previous demonic power.

The point that we no longer have a will is the point that we are no longer encountering the Holy Spirit. God has given us a free

will and at times will ask us to surrender our will to His, but "...
the spirits of the prophets are subject to the prophets."[3] There
is a fine line between surrender and giving up our free will.
We must keep that distinction clear and understand that it is
very important to remember where our freedom lies.[4] In other
words, the point where we give up our free will is the moment
that we are no longer choosing the freedom that Christ has
given us.

Our spiritual experiences must be placed in the hands of Jesus
himself, and only when He leads do we follow. We must be
careful about the degree to which we open ourselves up to an
encounter and allow ourselves to be given over. I was in a place
of allowing myself to be taken without really discerning who or
what was taking me, and it became a very dangerous spot.

It wasn't too long after this that a prophet friend of mine sent
me an email cautioning me and explaining what I had been
going through. She spoke of these "encounters" as a product of
the flesh. The reality is that when we begin to work these things
on our own accord, it is simply sorcery. Through this, the most
important lesson we can learn is that we have a choice in all
things. We must realize when we are in pursuit of Jesus that
He is the truest source of freedom. It is in him alone that we
experience the fullness of what God has for us. I share this not
to caution you in your pursuit of Him; I share it to caution you
in your motives of pursuit.

I say all of this to make this point: if you have had any history
in the occult or new age, get prayer for deliverance from any
residue. I was not actively pursuing power outside of Christ, but
I still had some residue. I needed some cleaning up. Deliverance

is a lifelong journey—I am not saying you will spend your life dealing with demons. But, in the world we live in, we can easily become offended, get hurt, etc., so following through with "maintenance" is important to keep ourselves clean.

The encounters I share with you in this book come from a clean place. I wouldn't share something I knew could be muddied—that would be too dangerous. I have also submitted it to other prophetic voices who have discerned, prayed, and made sure they should be released.

ENDNOTES

1. Acts 12:23
2. Psalm 104:4
3. 1 Corinthians 14:32
4. 2 Corinthians 3:17

CHAPTER FOUR

A BRAND-NEW ARM

August 2004

"And he touched his ear, and healed him." [1]

When I left the coven in June 2004 and was radically set on fire by God, I knew I needed to find a church home—a body to fellowship with. A family member was attending a denominational church in town, so I decided to give it a try. I was hungry and desperate for the move of God. I knew they spoke in tongues, so I figured I had nothing to lose. In spending time at this church, I was able to join their youth on a mission trip to Mexico. I had never been out of the country before, and I longed to see God show up. I am not saying here that God couldn't show up in America, but I knew from hearing the experiences of others that God indeed showed up when you went on a mission trip. As I mentioned earlier, I had done some itinerant ministry, but I had never been on a mission trip.

In the weeks leading up to the trzip, I sought God with a fervency and expectancy. I knew this would be another defining moment in my life. I longed to see God show up in a way that went beyond my experience. I had experienced the visitations, but I longed to see a real bonafide miracle. I left on the trip knowing that this would be one of those moments I would never forget.

I went on the trip, but immediately began to struggle with being there. I didn't really fit in with the other youth that went and I didn't know anyone at the mission base, so I found myself lonely and without a clue as to what to do. The trip seemed to drag on, and I began to doubt that God was going to show up.

Six days into the trip, I was beyond frustrated. While getting ready to head out for the day, I prayed this prayer, "Lord, aren't you going to do something? I'm all alone here with no friends and I still haven't seen your power at work. I really need you to do something, I don't care what it is, but I have to see you move today!"

And with that, we piled into the van and headed out to a little village. This is where things would change. This is where I met Laura.

Laura was about ten years old, and she was one of the little children running around the village. She had such a great smile, and her enthusiasm for our arrival went unrivaled. The thing about Laura was that she was different from all the other kids, and you definitely couldn't miss what made her stand out. You see, Laura only had one complete arm. Her left arm was marred and jagged where the doctors had to amputate it after a spider bite. She had been bitten a year and a half earlier and it became infected with gangrene (I learned all of this later). Despite her physical limitation, Laura was the happiest girl in the village and had no problem talking about her love for Jesus.

When I met Laura, it was as though my heart leapt. Somehow, I knew that this was going to be the miracle; I, of course, recognize now that it was God—*duh!* But in all seriousness, my heart was moved with compassion. I went to Laura, and I asked her in my broken Spanish if I could pray for her. She nodded yes and smiled the most beautiful smile. It was at this point that I didn't know what to do. I looked at the arm, so scarred and rough, and I said to it, "Arm! Grow! In Jesus' name!"

No one expected what happened next. Right through the rough and marred skin popped out a bone. This bone began to grow and grow until it splintered off, and the two bones that form the forearm were formed separately. From these two bones grew a skeletal hand; I watched as they formed right in front of my eyes. Behind the bones grew muscle and sinew and tendons, followed by skin. The miracle concluded with her finger nails growing to the same length as the other hand. Now the really cool part was that God even painted her finger nails to be the same color as the other hand. I realize some of you may be thinking, "Yeah right, God wouldn't do that—he wouldn't paint her nails." Yet it says in Psalms 37:23 that God delights in every detail of our lives.

Needless to say, after the minute and a half of the arm growing out, pandemonium broke out. The entire village went wild as people were crying, laughing, and praising God. Many people received healing that day in a little village in Mexico—it was incredible!

Healings broke out, people were saved, but the leaders of the team were upset. I couldn't figure out why none of them would talk to me, why they were angry with me, and when I finally did find out, it left me quite bewildered.

The leaders called me into the office when we arrived back in California and shared with me that I was not to share the testimony with anyone, because "God doesn't do stuff like that, and so it must be witchcraft." What?!? Witchcraft?!? I couldn't believe my ears. Having just come out of the coven and sought God for those months leading up to this huge breakthrough for my life, I couldn't believe that I was being accused of the very thing I had left. When I tried to explain the story to them, I was silenced and told that I would either keep it quiet or leave the church. I left.

I share this because a company of young people are rising out of the culture who are going to walk in miracles, signs, and wonders. Truth be told, some signs will make you wonder. But, we must be there to embrace and raise up a generation hungry for the reality of Heaven. It is our responsibility to steward them as we are stewards of God's mysteries.[2] Laura is now probably about 20 years old and is an evangelist in Mexico. She travels and shares the testimony of what God did, and people get healed all the time! Had someone written her off, she wouldn't be where she is today.

So, I charge you, expect the supernatural suddenlies of God, because He wants to break in. He wants to do the supernatural miracles that we so desperately need. When he does them, don't write them off.

TEACHING MOMENT:
CREATIVE MIRACLES

The Bible tells us that the same spirit that raised Jesus from the dead lives in us.[3] We have God's creative power working in us. The apostle John emphasized the creative power of the word working in the beginning of time, during the creation of the universe.

"In the beginning was the word, and the word was with God, and the word was God. He was in the beginning with God. All things were made through Him, and without Him nothing was made that was made."[4]

Can you see the power of the word? Jesus, the word, was in the beginning with God. All things were made through Him. Creation was released through what? Through the word of God. The scripture is clear—"without Him nothing was made that was made." God and His word are one. Creation is linked to His word. The apostle John again tells us the source of all created life:

"In Him was life, and the life was the light of men."[5]

However, as John points out, the world was only the beginning of God's creative work. With Jesus' life and death, the Father prepared the way for the creation of new spirits, of new creations in Christ,[6] and of spiritual sons and daughters.

"He was in the world, and the world was made through Him, and the world did not know Him. He came to His own, and His own did not receive Him. But as many as received Him, to them He gave the right to become children of God, to those who believe in His name: who were born, not of blood, nor of the will of the flesh, nor of the will of man, but of God."[7]

Today, God is still performing creative miracles, both inside His people and in the world through His people who have a revelation of His greatness and power. We want to be on the cutting edge and continue to study what it takes to be empowered with a creative miracle anointing.

Our authority is based on Jesus' victory. At the cross, Jesus as a man defeated satan and all demonic principalities, making a public spectacle of them before the audience of heaven, hell, and earth. This victory IS finished!

When He had disarmed the rulers and authorities [those

supernatural forces of evil operating against us], He made a public example of them [exhibiting them as captives in His triumphal procession], having triumphed over them through the cross.[8]

Our spiritual authority is based on our union with Jesus.[9] The power and benefits Jesus received as a man raised from the dead are given to us. God gave Jesus to the church as our head and made us His body to express his power to the earth.

We have been raised to sit with Jesus in heavenly places and are given access to God's throne. When we pray, we release the authority AND power based on our union with Christ. We must know who we are in Christ and the authority we possess in Jesus. We must take our place of authority in Christ as those seated in heavenly places with Jesus.[10]

Authority is a delegated power. A commonly used example is that of a police officer who stops a car by the authority of the government, not by his own physical power.

As Jesus' body, we are called to enforce His authority on the earth. As we walk in our identity rooted in him, those things that would try and hinder us are dethroned from our thinking, and we take on the Mind of Christ. Our authority is based on what Jesus accomplished, not on anything less.

If you search the entire New Covenant, you will find there is very little said about praying for the sick. As a matter of fact, I am only aware of one scripture that even uses the words praying for the sick, and that is James 5:15. All the other scriptures and examples we find in Jesus' ministry and that of the early church has to do more with using authority and speaking commands to be healed. Jesus never prayed to the Father asking Him to heal somebody, He spoke to the person and said something like, "Rise up and walk!" The early church did the same thing, except they added the name of Jesus. Peter didn't pray for the lame man to be healed, he spoke to the man, saying, "In the name of Jesus Christ of Nazareth rise up and walk."[11]

ENDNOTES

1. Luke 22:51
2. 1 Corinthians 14:1
3. Romans 8:11
4. John 1:1-3 (NKJV)
5. John 1:4 (NKJV)
6. II Corinthians 5:17
7. John 1:10-13 (NKJV)
8. Colossians 2:15 (AMP)
9. John 15
10. Ephesians 2:6
11. Acts 3:6

CHAPTER FIVE

MAMA JILL

July 2006 to January 2007

*"And, behold, there appeared unto them
Moses and Elias talking with him..."* [1]

In July of 2006, I met a woman named Jill Austin in a slightly less than conventional way. Jill Austin was the director of Master Potter Ministries and someone whom I have considered to be a spiritual mother. Jill passed into glory in January of 2009.

I met Jill in a dream. Yes, you read that correctly—a dream. In the dream, I had walked into an unfamiliar building, and Jill was sitting in a beautiful chair. She waved at me and motioned for me to come closer.

I asked her, "Who are you?"

"I'm Jill Austin. How are you today Jacob?"

The dream was so real, it was like I was truly there. As I stood there, she said in only a way Jill could, "Jacob, I have a word for you."

She stood up and placed her hand on my head, "Jacob, you have been called as a fire starter. You will carry great fire wherever you go, and you will live a lifestyle of visitation. The Lord has called you as a prophet in the earth to shift things in nations. You will have to take a stand in the hour to come, but know that you won't be defiled by ministry. God is going to use you to awaken the sleeping church."

I woke up from the dream shaking uncontrollably and wondering who this woman was. I wrote down the word that she gave me and held it in my heart.

Six months later, I was invited to attend a conference at a well-known church in southern California to hear a woman named Jill Austin. I didn't know who Jill was, and I hadn't taken the time to look her up. When I arrived on the campus, I began to feel like I had been there before. When I walked through the doors, I *knew* I had been there before. Upon crossing into the foyer, I looked to my left and there she was—Mama Jill. She was sitting just as she had been in the dream six months earlier. She waved at me and called out my name, "Jacob, come here."

My stomach was churning, as I knew this was the woman from my dream and here she was in front of me again. Moreover, she knew my name. She embraced me and said, "I forgot to give this to you the last time we met." She handed me her prayer shawl. She draped it around me and said, "This is for you." She handed me her card and said, "Call me any time, I will always be here for you." She hugged me again and said, "Don't forget that word I gave you. I have to run now, but call me this week." With that, she escaped down a hallway. I got to hear her speak several times that weekend and soaked it all in. It would be the last time

I would see her in person, though we had many conversations over the phone before she died.

I have long wondered about this experience and the significance of the prayer shawl. I thought for a while that it meant she gave me her mantle. What I realize now is that it was simply something the Lord had used to give me a part of what Jill carried.

We must push past the realm of human reasoning into the realm of God. God exists outside of time and space, and we are seated with Him— therefore, anything is possible. The Father is releasing a hunger into the body of Christ today. Are you hungry? Are you thirsty for more of God? This was one of Jill's favorite things to ask: "How hungry are you?" I ask you the same question today: How hungry are you? Do you want more of God? Are you willing to pay the price to encounter Him? As we lay our life down in complete surrender, I believe the Father is going to meet us in that place. The world needs us to bring the encounter. They are hungry and desperate for the answers that we hold.

In the place of complete surrender, we will begin to find ourselves living outside of the natural realm. We will find ourselves living in the supernatural. We will find ourselves living from the place that Jill lived, where the glory of God was so real to her, that everywhere she went the glory showed up in real, measurable realities.

Get ready for the reality of heaven to invade your space. Get ready to be caught up and taken into the lifestyle of encounters.

ENDNOTES

1. Matthew 17:3

CHAPTER SIX

DR. BRUCE

August 2007

"And it shall come to pass afterward, that I will pour out my spirit upon all flesh; and your sons and your daughters shall prophesy, your old men shall dream dreams, your young men shall see visions." [1]

From the time, I was a little boy I have had dreams from the Lord, but I rarely understood what they meant. I would dream of heaven or about events that had not happened yet. These dreams would sometimes scare me simply because I didn't understand them.

At the time of this encounter, I was part of the worship team at my church, so during the worship time, I was on stage leading with the team. It was an amazing night of worship. We had a visiting prophet named Bruce. During worship, I couldn't help but look over at him. I had never met someone of his nature. He seemed like a rather peculiar fellow (most prophets are), with a very bright green and blue striped shirt, blue jeans, and burnt-mustard cowboy boots. He had graying hair with a school-boy cut, round little beady eyes, and wire-rimmed glasses.

Trying not to lose focus, I re-centered my attention on the Lord. The song service was soon over, and I left the stage to sit in the same seat I had always sat in—the center set of chairs, front row, last chair on the right. My pastor introduced Dr. Bruce. He got up and chose not to use the pulpit to preach but rather spoke from our level. I remember him describing the characteristics of the third day church and then he moved on to talking about quantum physics and its role in the supernatural. It was all quite amazing, and I was very enthralled with everything he spoke about.

Then he began to talk about the prophetic and the way that it can change your life. It was then that he said, "One word from God can change your life!" That statement still rings in my ears today, and I will never forget it. He closed his teaching with a quick prayer and then invited us all up to the front for prayer and words of prophecy.

After a long while, Dr. Bruce reached me, and this is what he said, "You have had dreams since a very young age and don't know what they mean, right?"

I replied, "Yes! I have."

He said, "Well God wants you to know that He has given you those dreams. He has set you as a watchman on the wall, just like it says in Isaiah 62:6. You are going to have dreams at a more rapid rate than you have in the past. God is going to give you dreams for yourself, for others, and even for the nation. Don't take this lightly, it is very vital that you are obedient to the Lord and write them down. You need to write each and every one of them down. Don't broadcast them to the world, yet! God has a timing and season for you to share them with others, and you will be a mighty servant of Him in the times to come. Rely on His Spirit, and allow Him to speak to you."

I broke down and cried. I hadn't really told anyone about my dreams, and when he said those words, I felt like God validated me. I knew at that moment, that I wasn't crazy and that I was really hearing the Lord.

TEACHING MOMENT:
IMPORTANCE OF INTERPRETING DREAMS

There are many of you out there who have had dreams, visions, and encounters that you haven't been able to share with anyone. I want you to know that God validates you! He sees you! Begin to ask Him for strategy and ask Him what to do and watch as He speaks to you!

A wise person once explained the importance of dreams to me in this way:

"Dreams are the perfect way to hear from God. When you are dreaming, you are quiet, so you can't ignore Him. Plus, you are not easily distracted. You're basically all ears for about seven hours every night."

Personal experience has confirmed this notion. On many occasions, the Lord has spoken powerful words of encouragement and warning while I slept. Through biblical study, I have found that God intends to speak to each of His followers in this manner. In fact, the prophet Joel foretold of a time when God's Spirit would compel us to dream:[2] "I will pour out my Spirit upon all people. Your sons and daughters will prophesy. Your old men will dream dreams, and your young men will see visions."[3]

Further confirmation of God speaking through dreams to His children is found in the book of Job. In Chapter 33, Job is confronted with the reality of God's voice in our lives—whether we hear it or not.

For God speaks again and again, though people do not recognize it. He speaks in dreams, in visions of the night, and when deep sleep falls on people as they lie in their beds. He whispers in their ears...[4]

It's important to understand that not all dreams are God-given. It may be that you ate something weird, or that your mind just kept going after a busy day. Dreams can also be from Satan. The enemy of our souls isn't ignorant of the power of visions. Let I Samuel 28 be a warning. It recounts a time when King Saul seeks counsel from a medium.

HOW TO HANDLE VIVID DREAMS

1. Pray. Before you do anything else, pray that God exposes the source of a dream and what He wants to teach you through it.

2. Listen to God. Take a moment and sit quietly before the Lord so that you may hear His perspective. Once you feel His peace, then you can rest assured that His Spirit was the source. Hearing from the Lord can save you as it did the three wise men. They were warned in a dream to return home another way, avoiding King Herod, and in turn saving the newborn Jesus.[5]

3. Write it down. Grab a notebook and write down what you remember. If, after praying, you feel that the dream isn't of the Lord, then forget about it. But if you think God is in it, journal what you feel He is speaking to you.

4. Seek godly counsel. Sharing dreams is biblical. Pharaoh sought wise counsel from Joseph and a generation was saved from starvation.[6] Just be wise about with whom you share your visions. Be especially cautious of friends who consult books to interpret dreams.[7] Often, these books and philosophies leave God out of the equation altogether.

5. Let it be. The Lord will bring His dreams to your remembrance. Most of my dreams are extremely vivid, but the ones I pay closest attention to are the ones I remember years after having them. Occasionally, while sitting in God's presence, He will recall a dream to my mind to reinforce a lesson He is teaching me. The danger comes when the dream preoccupies our thoughts instead of the One who gives us these supernatural visions.

ENDNOTES

1. Joel 2:28

2. Acts 2

3. Joel 2:28 (NLT)

4. Job 33:14-16a (NLT)

5. Matthew 2

6. Genesis 41

7. I John 4:1

CHAPTER SEVEN
THE TWIRLING INTERCESSORS

October 2007

"Then the spirit took me up..." [1]

I was part of an intercessory prayer team at my home church in Dinuba, California. Every Tuesday night, myself and about 10-12 others would gather to pray. On this particular night, we were deep in intercession for our church and city. The presence of God was so thick and tangible.

At some point during our prayer time, there was a shift in the room. Something had changed, and the presence of the Lord was stronger than it had been. It was as if we had pierced the veil that separated earth and heaven. We were standing in a circle holding hands and were to the left side of the room, when suddenly it felt like we were no longer on the ground.

All at once, we opened our eyes to find that not only were we no longer on the left side of the room, but we had been completely moved to the other side of the room and had rotated 180 degrees! Each one of us stood dumbfounded, shocked and trying to figure out if what had just happened really did happen.

It was then that one of the intercessors spoke up and said, "Did anyone else feel like we were in a whirlwind?" Pretty much in unison, the answer was an emphatic "YES!" We entered a time of worship and were so thankful that as a group we could experience the Lord of the Whirlwinds.

TEACHING MOMENT:
FIGHTING FOR UNITY

As the body of Christ begins to walk in unity, they will begin to experience these types of encounters together. God desires to move among his people in these ways, simply to establish the spirit of unity in the church. As the church manifests the kingdom, wild and sometimes unexplainable occurrences take place. This wasn't the first time or the last time that God showed up in our prayer meetings. There has to be militancy and a fight inside of us saying, "Yes, Lord. I want to know You! Yes, Lord, I am going to fight for my family. I am going to fight for my children. I am going to fight for my husband. I am going to fight for my friends." There must be tenacity and a warring spirit in a warring Bride that says, "Yes Lord, I want more of you!"

You need to cry out, "Lord, I want to have such a radical touch from You, because Lord, I want You to touch my family, my husband, my children, and my loved ones." There has to be a cry in you for a radical touch of His Spirit.

We must break apathy to get to the hunger and fight inside of your spirit. There should be a cry inside of your spirit, a roar, that you want more of God! We love you, Lord! You are the King of Kings and the Lord of Glory! Jesus, we love You radically and intimately!

As you seek the Lord together, watch and see what will happen.

ENDNOTES

1. Ezekiel 3:12

CHAPTER EIGHT

MESSENGERS OF PROVISION: GRACE AND JOY

October 2008

"And as he lay and slept under a juniper tree, behold, then an angel touched him, and said unto him, arise and eat…" [1]

In October of 2008, while attending a ministry school in northern California, I had taken a trip south to Monterey, California, to visit a friend of mine going to school there. At the time, I was really struggling financially and probably shouldn't have made the trip, but on the way back to Redding, I had an encounter that would forever change the way I would view the provision of the Lord.

As I was driving up the I-5 headed back towards Redding, I pulled off to grab a bite to eat at a fast food place. I got out of my car, and as I was walking into the restaurant, I noticed two elderly ladies sitting outside the door. I thought to myself, "If they are out here when I come back I will see if they need a ride." Well, sure enough, they were.

I approached them and asked them if they needed a ride. I explained that I was headed to Redding and would be more than happy to take them that way. I need to explain, these were the most unique older ladies I had ever seen. The first lady had short burgundy hair that was permed very tightly to her head. She wore dark lipstick and had an oversized brown fur coat that swallowed her tiny frame. The second lady was more robust, with shoulder length grey hair. and she too had a large fur coat on. She, however, didn't speak a word to me. I thought to myself, these are some peculiar ladies wearing fur coats in 85-degree October weather.

The first lady said they would "love a ride" and that they were "headed to Redding as well." So off we went. They got into my car, the smaller one sitting in front while the silent one took the backseat. We had been driving for about an hour when the lady in the back seat began to sing. Mind you, we had been riding in silence for that entire hour. I had tried to put the radio on at one point and was asked to keep the car quiet. At first, I was a bit perturbed by the silence, but there was a sense of peace about these women. It was because of the peace they carried that I decided I could endure the deafening silence. So, when she began to sing, I knew this was more than just happenstance. This was an encounter.

The lady began to sing the following,

> "Jacob, you are called.
> Jacob, you are destined.
> Jacob, you have a good Father.
> Jacob, you are meant for so much more.
> Jacob, trust your Father.
> Jacob, He will provide for you."

She sang these same words over and over. It was the most beautiful thing I had ever heard. I took an exit into a rest stop and just sat there and cried as she was singing these words. She sang them over and over as she placed her hand on my shoulder.

Then the lady in the front seat spoke up. When she spoke, chills ran down my spine as the tangible presence of the Lord had filled the car. She said, "Jacob, fret not little one. Your Father has heard your cries of desperation. You must trust Him for provision, He will truly meet all of the needs you have."

I sat there and cried and cried. What they said spoke right to my heart. I had been struggling so hard to believe that God was my provider, and here these sweet ladies had spoken to the very cry of my heart.

The lady in the backseat then said, "Jacob, this is our stopping point, we must go now, but you must never forget this. You must always remember that the Lord sent us here just for you."

I replied, "But I must know your names! Who are you?"

The lady sitting in front said as she was getting out of the car, "I am Grace, and she is Joy." I didn't want them to get out of the car, and so I said, "But this is just a rest stop, can't I take you all the way to Redding?" Grace responded, "No, this is where we depart. You'll be fine, sweet boy." She shut the car door. Together they walked off into the grass and before my very eyes, they were gone.

Poof! In an instant, the two sweet ladies whom I thought were strange little women were gone. Were they angels? No! They were high level intercessors.

I sat in my car for a few minutes, completely dumbfounded at what had just happened but knowing I would never forget it. As I sat reflecting in the car, I heard the Lord say, "Jacob, it is in my grace and joy that you will find provision. Joy is the outflow of trust, and grace is the standard by which I provide."

How profound is that? Joy is the outflow of trust. As we begin to trust in the Lord, we will find ourselves in a place of joy. Stress and worry only come in when we are outside of trust. If God provides for the sparrow, will he not provide for us? Then, when we look at grace as the standard by which he provides, we realize He will always go above and beyond to take care of His children. If grace is His unmerited favor, that is a huge standard of provision.

I pray that you will receive his grace and joy today and that from that place you will begin to walk in unmerited favorable provision for everything you have need of. I pray that you will come to understand the j oy the Father has in providing for you and that His grace is sufficient for every situation you may face.

TEACHING MOMENT:
THERE ARE NO FEMALE ANGELS IN SCRIPTURE

Some people have asked, were these angels? I made the mistake in the first printing of this book of calling them angels, I am taking time to correct this here. It needs to be understood that there are no female angels in the Bible. There is much deception that needs to be cleared up in this area. Most of the angels seen on television, in gift shops, on greeting cards, book covers, the Internet, Christmas decorations, etc., are female angels. However, this is not in accordance with Scripture. I do not call the women who showed up "angels"—they were high level intercessors who were transported from another region to me.

When God finally responded to thirty-seven chapters of complaining by Job and his friends, He confirmed, at the same time, that the angels of God are men, not women.

"Then the Lord answered Job out of the whirlwind, and said ... where wast thou when I laid the foundations of the Earth ... when the morning stars sang together, and all the sons of God shouted for joy?"[2]

The original Hebrew word for "sons" in this verse is a masculine noun.

So it is clear that the angels of God whom God refers to as "the sons of God" are male in nature, not female.

In Psalm 103, the Bible also clearly says that the angels of God are "all powerful men."

"Bless the Lord, ye His angels, that excel in strength, that do His commandments, hearkening unto the voice of His word."[3]

In the original Hebrew "that excel in strength" actually says "all powerful men." The word "men" here is a masculine noun, and it is the only way angels are described in the Bible.

Although in the Scripture, angels are always and only referred to as "men," some angels are so beautiful in appearance that to the natural, human, untrained eye, they can appear to be women.

Again, angels never appear as females in the Bible, which clearly says they are "all-powerful men."

Some have said that the two women in the book of Zechariah 5:9-11 are angels. However, these are not angels at all. Rather, they are demonic instruments in God's hands sent to bring judgment to the nation of Israel by bringing them once again into captivity, as a result of their sins against Him.

Most all scholars, commentators, and translators agree that these two "women" are evil spirits and that the "wind in their wings" denotes the swiftness with which they would bring judgment to Israel.

The Apostle Paul said we must not remain children in knowledge, being tossed to and fro by every false doctrine that comes down the pike.

ENDNOTES

1. 1 Kings 19:5
2. Job 38:1-7; see also Job 1:6 and 2:1
3. Psalm 103:20

CHAPTER NINE
JESUS RETURNS
March 2009

"I will manifest myself to him..." John 14:21" [1]

In March of 2009, while attending a ministry school in Northern California, we had a day where our assignment was to get out of our norm and "encounter the Lord." I woke up that morning with great expectation of what was going to happen. I knew that to take full advantage of this day, I would have to get out of the house, and so I did. I got in my car, and when the Lord said turn left, I would turn left. When He said turn right, I would turn right. I ended up in the mountains outside of Redding. I found a side road that seemed to lead to a walking trail and parked. I took the long trek until I finally reached a clearing. I was near a river and dam that I didn't even know existed.

As I was walking along the river, I found a huge rock and had the thought, "I will lie down like Jacob did at Beth-El." I hadn't been lying there more than five minutes when I heard someone call my name. To be perfectly honest, I was annoyed. I thought to myself, "How in the world did someone find me all the way out here?" I had definitely thought I would be alone. So, begrudgingly, I sat up and looked around but saw no one. I heard my name again. It was coming from across the river. It was there I noticed a man waving at me, and at first, I didn't recognize who it was. He started coming toward me, and once he hit the water, and he didn't sink... I knew *exactly* who it was. It was the *One* who had first encountered me thirteen years earlier. Now I cannot say for sure that others would have seen him, but I cannot deny that I did.

He strode swiftly across the water and was at my side within seconds. Here He was looking at me with those same passion-filled eyes; the very lover of my soul! He knelt beside me and kissed me on the forehead. His very presence was overwhelming! We were locked in a gaze that, while only lasting a few seconds, seemed like an eternity.

He spoke, "Jacob, I have come to do something very important. Your heart has been tainted and abused the last several months. I have come to remove what shouldn't be there, and in exchange I will give you my heart. This may be painful, but it will be worth it. Lie back down on the rock."

I was immediate in my obedience. I laid down upon the rock. He pulled my shirt up and I watched as his hand began to cut down my chest. He started at my neck and ended at my navel. He had made an incision using his finger, which began to sting slightly. My skin had been gingerly sliced open. He then cut into my sternum and popped open my rib cage. Right before my eyes, I was watching the Lord literally give me open-heart surgery. There wasn't much pain at first, but the longer my chest was open, the more pain there seemed to be. From time to time, He would reach over and brush his hand across my brow to bring me comfort.

He then reached into my chest and pulled out my blackened, barely beating heart. In one swift move, He reached into His own chest and pulled out His heart. His heart was red and full of life; I could feel the pulsating beat even before he placed it in my chest. He said, "I am making a divine exchange, I will take your messy, broken heart, and in return I will give you mine. But… You must learn to protect your heart Jacob, for out of it comes all of the issues of life."[2]

When He placed His heart into my chest, I felt life flow through me like never before. It was intense! There was a very soothing yet uncomfortable feeling that came with it. The feeling was tolerable, but it was very unnerving. I had never felt life like this before, and all of sudden, the weight of what it meant to protect my heart had just become real. He then closed me up. He pulled flesh from his side, and He rolled it out like putty before putting it over the wound. It matched perfectly, to the point that you couldn't tell there had been a scar there. He took my blackened, broken heart and He put it inside of himself. He said, "I take messy, broken hearts and make something beautiful out of them. Let's take a walk."

Jesus next looked at me and said, "My time is up. I must go now, but remember this Jacob—if I provide for the birds, I will provide for you." Jesus embraced me and held me tight. He again kissed my forehead, and with these words, He was gone: "You are loved."

This was the last time I saw Him in this fashion. There have been many times, however, that I have seen His similitude in the room and sensed His presence so very near. I honestly long for the day when I will see Him in this way again, but I also know it will be in His perfect timing.

TEACHING MOMENT:
HOW TO ENGAGE WITH GOD

There are times in our life when we experience intimate moments with the Lord. During these times, it is important to realize that Jesus desires to reveal Himself to us more clearly, and we must focus all our attention on Him in order to receive the message He desires to convey to us.

In the gospel of Matthew, we see the account of the Lord's transfiguration. Jesus had only chosen Peter, James, and John to go up on the mountain with him to experience this special moment. While on the mountain, Peter, James, and John watched, as they saw the Lord's face begin to shine like the sun and His clothes became dazzling white. Suddenly, Moses and Elijah appeared and began talking with Jesus. The original Greek language implies that this conversation Jesus had with Moses and Elijah was not brief, but rather somewhat lengthy. Peter made a mistake by thinking that Moses and Elijah were somehow on the same level with Jesus, so he offered to build three tent shelters, one for Jesus, one for Moses, and one for Elijah. While Peter was suggesting this idea, a luminescent cloud overshadowed them, and a voice spoke out of the cloud, saying, "This is my Son, whom I love; with him I am well pleased. Listen to him!"[4]

It's important to keep our focus on Jesus and not let other things distract us. We need to listen to what the Lord has to say and not be mesmerized by someone else's name or persona. Once you've met the Lord, there is no higher level to ascend to. Every knee bows to Jesus, and He is Lord over all. This doesn't mean we don't esteem the Lord's ministers, and I certainly don't want to imply that. It just means we must keep things in context, especially when the Lord is present. Peter put his foot in his mouth at the wrong time because he had probably heard about Moses and Elijah all his life, since he was Jewish. Now, when he saw them in person, he was ecstatic. But the focus was to be on Jesus. It reminds me of the time Jesse Duplantis went to heaven and met the Lord Jesus in person. He said it was an awesome experience, and that he lay before the Lord on his face because of the glory of God. Shortly after that, while still in heaven, he met King David, and Jesse said he bowed on his knees when he met King David. But he said David corrected him and told him to stand up. David explained to Jesse that he had just met Jesus, the King of Kings, and that because of that he did not need to bow to any other man. After the voice thundered from the cloud, we see the focus of the apostles put in proper order.

When the disciples heard this, they fell facedown to the ground, terrified. But Jesus came and touched them. "Get up," he said, "Don't be afraid." When they looked up they saw no one except Jesus."[5]

During a visitation, we must listen intently to what Jesus has to say and keep our focus on Him. I believe the statement, "When they looked up, they saw no one except Jesus" has a dual meaning. Yes, the open vision had ended, and no one else was around, but it also implies they esteemed the Lord much higher than they ever had before. Their focus was now directly on Jesus, who is the center of attention. We see another example in the scriptures that helps us know how to conduct ourselves when the Lord is present. After the resurrection, Peter had been talking with Jesus, and the Lord asked Peter three times if Peter loved Him. This was a deep cleansing session taking place within Peter. Peter had denied the Lord three times during the hours leading up to the crucifixion. Now that Jesus was resurrected and raised triumphant, He was reversing the curses Peter brought upon himself by asking Peter three times if he loved Him. This act closed all doors to the enemy concerning having future access to Peter. After such a remarkable moment, we then read that

"Peter turned and saw that the disciple whom Jesus loved was following them. (This was the one who had leaned back against Jesus at the supper and had said, "Lord, who is going to betray you?") When Peter saw him, he asked, "Lord, what about him?" Jesus answered, "If I want him to remain alive until I return, what is that to you? You must follow me."[6]

It displeased the Lord that Peter *turned around* in the middle of the conversation. That is a big "no no" with the Lord. When we are in the presence of the Lord and God is speaking to us, it is not the time to answer a phone call. We can always call someone back once the Lord is finished. He desires our undivided attention when He is speaking to us. Jesus basically told Peter that he did not need to be concerned about what was going to happen to John. That was none of his business. Peter needed to focus on his own calling, and the person with all the answers was standing right next to him.

Visions, trances, and heavenly experiences are usually events that require us leaning into the flow. We can pull out if we choose by being distracted or by not believing in faith. We are living in a supernatural dispensation of time where visitations are coming, and I felt it important to share a little on proper spiritual etiquette. Be prepared for when the Lord chooses to speak to you. He has good things to say, and we don't want to miss a single word.

ENDNOTES

1. John 14:21
2. Proverbs 4:23
3. Psalm 16:11
4. Matthew 17:5 (NIV)
5. Matthew 17:6 (NIV)
6. John 21:20-22 (NIV)

CHAPTER 10

THE ISSACHAR UNDERSTANDING

April 2009

"And of the children of Issachar, which were men that had understanding of the times, to know what Israel ought to do..."[1]

In April of 2009, I had the following encounter. It is probably one of the most profound things I have ever experienced and one that has taken me a long time to wrap my head around. It is the encounter that has carried the heaviest burden for me.

I was awakened at about 3:00 am with a knock on my door. My roommates were gone on their respective mission trips, and I was alone in my room. I lived in a house where there were people always in and out with several young children, so it wasn't uncommon for someone to be knocking on my door. However, at 3:00 am, I was rather annoyed by the knock. I arose from my bed and opened the door, where I was blinded by an intensely bright light.

It took several seconds for my eyes to adjust to the light, and when they did, I was standing in front of a group of about 30 older men. These men were dressed in very ancient Jewish garb, much like that of the high priests mentioned in the book of Exodus. They had the linen turban with a plate of pure gold adorning the front of it. There was the linen ephod of blue, purple, scarlet, and gold with the breastplate of judgment, which contained four rows of stone in settings of gold. The top row had a red sardius stone, a yellow topaz, and a reddish carbuncle. The next row had an emerald, a sapphire and a diamond. Following this was a yellowish ligure, a sparkling agate, and an amethyst. Finally, the bottom row contained beryl, onyx, and jasper. Upon their shoulders were two onyx stones, which had engraved upon them the names of the 12 tribes of Israel.

I stood before these men, bewildered at their unannounced visitation. Then, one by one, they filed past me into my bedroom. Now, for a group this size to fit into my tiny bedroom was a sight to see! They filled every nook and cranny. Some sat on my roommate's bed, and some stood in the doorway to the bathroom. I gingerly pushed my way through the crowd to my bed, where I took a seat, still not having exchanged any words with these men.

They were all staring at me, which was honestly making me feel quite uncomfortable. Finally, after what seemed an eternity, one of the men spoke up. He said, "Greetings young prophet. I am Tola, and we are the Sons of Issachar. We have come on an assignment from Yahweh to release to you the "Understanding of the Times and Seasons" that He has bestowed upon us. For many years, the Lord has required of us to release this upon men, and yet, very few have taken this understanding and cherished it. Many have used it for their own gain and wealth. You must carry this understanding with great caution and great discernment. You must learn to seek the Lord for His timing in situations. You will not be permitted to share this understanding with many, but you do have permission to release an impartation of the Issachar Understanding."

I sat there as he spoke to me, feeling the reverential fear of the Lord. I could feel the weight of this moment. I was lost in thought about all of this when I suddenly realized that he had stopped talking as he noticed my distraction. I looked at him and apologized, "I am so sorry! I can just feel the weight of what you are sharing, and I don't know if I can carry this gift that is being placed before me."

Tola replied, "The Lord would not have sent us here if He did not trust you with it. Standing before you are the eldest of the sons of Issachar. These are men who have discerned situations for Israel and have shared wisdom for ages. What comes with the understanding is the weight of discernment of knowing when to share direction and when not to share it. What we bring before you today is heaven's timepiece."

He then placed in my hand a small gold watch. It did not have straps, and it did not seem to run like a normal clock. Rather, the watch was set at 12:00, with the second hand 10 seconds from 12:00. He said, "When the clock begins to tick again, you will know the season has truly shifted for the church." I still have heaven's timepiece to this day, and I await the day that it begins ticking again.

He then directed another man to step forward. This man spoke, "Greetings Jacob. I am Phuvah, and I too am a son of Issachar. I am also the keeper of the timelines. What I am about to give you has only been given to a few select men. You are to guard these with your life, and when the time comes, they will be revealed to you." He then began to unfurl several pieces of parchment. I began to look at them, but I did not understand what they said. I took them in my hands, and as I did, they disappeared. There have been several instances over the last several years where I have dreamt of these scrolls and seen little pieces revealed to me. I do not yet know what these scrolls mean in their entirety but have received bits and pieces from time to time.

About the time the scrolls disappeared, another man stepped forward. He was very stoic and did not have much expression when he spoke. "Jacob, for centuries, men have longed to have the understanding that we have had, but they have not desired it for the right reasons. I must warn you that the gift of understanding comes with a price, and you must be ready to carry this weight, remembering that you are not the gift. The gift comes only from the source of life—the Father. What I am about to give to you is a set of maps. These maps will show the pockets of God's glory that have rested on the Earth, and they will show you the plan for worldwide revival. They will also reveal to you the pockets of darkness, the literal strongholds on the earth."

"You must never use this for your own gain, and you must never allow others to exploit this. You will be called upon to share the revelation with many, but do not allow them to exploit it." With this warning, he handed me several maps. As I gazed upon the maps, I was shocked to see that places I had viewed as hubs of glory were not marked, and the places I had expected to see the most darkness were actually sparkling with the beginnings of the moves of God."

Tola spoke again, "Jacob, tonight is a shifting moment for you. From this night forward, you will walk in great discernment of the times and seasons. You will have a period following this that will seem like you lack complete discernment, but trust that in the precise moment, your discernment will explode. Phuvah, please place the ephod upon him."

At this point, I was asked to stand, and they placed a beautiful garment upon me. Phuvah spoke, "You will be used to raise up a company of priestly prophets, who know what it is to weep before the Lord. They will know what it is to minister to the Lord, and from that place, prophesy into existence the very will of God."

As he finished speaking, the other men began to pass by me, and as they did, they would place their hands upon my shoulders, and bless me in their Hebrew tongue. Finally, the very stoic man who had spoken earlier reached me, looked straight into my eyes, and spoke these words, "Son, prophesy, prophesy, prophesy. Speak, speak, speak. Know, know, know." He blew upon my face, and as he did, a fire consumed me. It was a heat I had never felt before, and I could feel it burning into my very being. It was the sealing of that which was the Lord, and the cleansing that Isaiah spoke about in Isaiah 6.

Tola again spoke, "You have now received the Issachar Understanding. Guard it, protect it, and use it wisely, young prophet." With that, the men began to file past me again, and this time each one embraced me as they filed out the door. Tola, Phuvah, and the very stoic man were all that remained. The man spoke, "We will meet again, this is not the last time you will see us." With that, they walked out the door. To this day, I still don't know who the unnamed man is.

TEACHING MOMENT:
THE ISSACHAR ANOINTING

For some, this encounter may seem strange, and the truth is that *it is* strange. I would not call these types of encounters a "regular occurrence," by any means. But I believe these are the types of things that are happening across the earth. God is releasing encounters to those who are ready to receive them. I encourage you to seek the Lord not only for encounters, but for the Issachar Understanding. God wants you to know the times and the seasons, so you may minister effectively in the days ahead.

The children of Issachar were men who "understood the times, to know what Israel ought to do." The Hebrew word for "understanding," "bee-nah," has a root which also means discernment, wisdom, perception, and knowledge.

We live in a day and age in which discernment is a sorely needed gift in the body of Christ—and praise God, it's a gift which is freely given by the Holy Spirit![1]

Why? Because the enemy of our souls is cunning and subtle, and a major sign of the times is the proliferation of "seducing spirits" and "doctrines of devils."[2]

A.W. Tozer once stated, "The red corpuscles are like faith—they carry the life-giving oxygen to every part of the body. The white cells are like discernment—they pounce upon dead and toxic matter and carry it out to the drain. In a healthy heart, there must be provision for keeping dead and poisonous matter out of the life stream."

So how can we become like the children of Issachar? By building up our spiritual immune system. We need to ask for and develop the spiritual gift of discernment, not falling into the trap of spiritual laziness where we fail to discern truth from error, or to identify the enemy's spiritual toxins which could poison us.

Let's ask God for this important gift! Let's ask the spirit of truth to lead and guide us with discernment, every step of the way so that we become like the children of Issachar—able to understand the times and to know what we ought to do!

ENDNOTES

1. 1 Corinthians 12:10
2. 1 Timothy 4:1

CHAPTER ELEVEN

ROMANIAN TRANSLATION

October 2009

"...the Spirit of the Lord caught away Philip..." [1]

I remember the night like yesterday. I was sitting in my room worshipping. By this time, I was back in my parent's house in Dinuba, California, after attending ministry school in Redding. I was lost in worship when I heard the Lord say, "Open your eyes." When I opened my eyes, I was looking directly into my closet. I had to rub my eyes because the closet looked fuzzy. I couldn't figure out what was going on, so I got off the bed and walked to the closet for a closer inspection.

As I got closer to the closet, I could still see my clothes, but in front of them was this strange, almost gelatin-like substance. I reached my hand up to it, and as I touched it, my fingers disappeared inside of it. I recoiled my hand in utter disbelief. I reached back in, and once again, my hand disappeared. I did this several times until I heard the Lord say, "Go!" I immediately knew what this meant—I was supposed to go through this "portal." So, that's what I did! I stepped into the closet and immediately found myself in another place. I had been transported! This wasn't just a spiritual movement; my physical body was *literally* transported to another place!

I looked around to gather my surroundings. I wasn't entirely sure where I was, but it seemed very foreign. There were some pastures ahead of me, and behind me was a small village. As I turned around, I could see in the distance some of the people running to what I could only make out to be a hut of some sort that had caught fire. I followed the people to the hut. As I was on my way, I saw a little sign that said welcome to Voslabeni, Romania. As I got closer to the village, I realized I was correct in believing that I had seen a hut on fire. The people had gathered around it.

I began to ask what was happening, but no one understood what I was saying. As a matter of fact, they seemed quite curious as to who I was. I heard the Lord say, "Speak to them in a way they would understand." I didn't know what this meant, but the first thing that came to mind was to speak to them in a Romanian accent. So, that is what I did. I mustered up my best Romanian accent and asked what was happening. They began to speak back to me in their native tongue, which I suddenly understood.

They were screaming, "The little girl! The little girl! She is stuck inside!" I asked, "What is her name?" They replied, "Ileana." I immediately felt the prompting of the Lord to go into the burning hut. So, without fear, I rushed into the fire.

I couldn't see very well, but I called out her name, "Ileana, are you there? Where are you sweetie? I have come to help you." I didn't hear anything as I made my way through this burning hut. Finally, I heard a small cry coming from the back corner. As I made my way closer, I realized that she was stuck underneath a rather large beam. It was crushing her diaphragm, so she was unable to really cry out for help. I could hear the people on the outside screaming for her.

I made my way toward her, and as I did, I cried out to the Lord, "You are going to have to help me lift this Lord." Parts of the wood were charred, and some had burning embers. I grabbed onto it with all of my strength and lifted. As I did, I cried out, "Jeesssuuusss! Jeesssuuusss!!!" I was able to lift the beam off of her. I had burnt my hand, and there was ash all over me. I grabbed Ileana and told her that she was going to be okay. I rushed out of the hut with her in my arms, and as we made it out of the building, it suddenly collapsed behind us. The villagers responded with great shouts of joy!

As I handed her over to her mom, the villagers asked me where I had come from. I proceeded to tell them that I had been sent by the Lord Jesus. I told them how He saves, and I gave them the simple gospel message. I asked how many of them wanted to receive the Lord who had sent me to them. There wasn't a hand that didn't go up; I led them all to the Lord!

I then asked them if they wanted to receive His Spirit. Again, every hand went up. That day, at least 30 Romanians were saved and filled with the Holy Ghost, all because I was obedient to step through something with which I was very unfamiliar. I ministered in healing to the crowd, and several miracles broke out. One lady even received her sight back.

Upon finishing the "altar call," I saw the portal reappear behind the crowd. I knew that it was time to leave. I told them the Lord would send people to teach them about Him, and with that, I stepped back through the portal and was back in my bedroom. I looked down at my hands, and they were still covered in ash and while my hand was burned, it wasn't painful. As a matter of fact, it healed quite quickly over the next couple of days.

TEACHING MOMENT:
SUPERNATURAL TRANSLATIONS
& TRANSPORTATIONS

Ezekiel was transported in the spirit and describes the experience in Ezekiel 8. He was moved from his dwelling place outside Israel during the captivity and taken some distance to Jerusalem. Phillip experienced a similar thing after baptizing the Ethiopian eunuch.[2] Paul described his trip to heaven, confessing he didn't know if he was there only in the spirit or in his physical body.[3]

While friends were interceding for Peter, he was mysteriously freed by an angel. It's obvious he didn't know if it was a vision or an experience in the natural.[4] After traveling through a gate, which opened by itself, he arrived at home. Someone made the comment that it wasn't Peter, but his angel, which begs the question, were people known to have experiences in which angels appeared as friends and family? Much of the book of Revelation is an account of the things John saw and heard while being taken to different places in the spirit realm and in the natural.

Jesus was often slipping away and reappearing mysteriously. He appeared walking on water.[5] He disappeared after talking with the two disciples he met on the road to Emmaus and re-appeared to a different group shortly after.[6] He appeared to the disciples again in a room where the doors were closed, which seems to imply he either walked through a wall or materialized before them.[7] Jesus also made a fascinating comment about the fact that we would do the things he did: "Most assuredly, I say to you, he who believes in Me, the works that I do he will do also; and greater works than these he will do, because I go to My Father.[8]

There's plenty of scriptural backing behind transportation in the spirit. One could even argue that Jesus wanted us to do the very things he did and more. But some stumble at these ideas. The word says, "to those who believe, all things are possible."

There will be times in the days ahead that much ministry will be done in this way. God will send you places not by your own power or might, but through His spirit. It has been prophesied that in the last days, Christians will no longer use normal modes of transportation, but will be translated and transported across the world. Get ready to go!

ENDNOTES

1. Acts 8:39
2. Acts 8:39
3. 2 Cor. 12:2
4. Acts 12:8-10
5. Matthew 14:25
6. Luke 24:31-36
7. John 20:26
8. John 14:12

CHAPTER TWELVE

THE ANGEL WITH THE MANTLE CALLED AWAKENING

April 2016

*"Elijah took his mantle and folded it together
and struck the waters." 2 Kings 2:8*

I was sitting in my living room preparing for a meeting that I was to speak at later in the evening. I heard the Lord clearly say, "Prepare yourself for an encounter." I assumed He was speaking of the meeting. I began to worship, and immediately the atmosphere shifted. Through the front door entered an angel. He was about seven-and-a-half feet tall. He carried in his hands a very large tallit.

He said, "I am the angel with the mantle called 'Awakening.'"

Instantly, I went from my living room and into an open vision where I saw the angel stretching the mantle over people and dropping it on them. One by one, they came and stood under the mantle, and it would drop on them.

I was reminded of Elijah when he threw his mantle upon Elisha. It was the same principle here. This angel was throwing his mantle on people who were willing to receive it.

There were others who stood by and watched, "oohing" and "aahing" at the activity of the angel, but they didn't draw near. The angel spoke to me: "They love the atmosphere, but they don't like the cost of getting out of their comfort to possess it."

The Lord then spoke and said, "There will be those who possess the mantle, there will be those who will avoid the mantle, and then there will be those who attempt to abuse the mantle."

BREAKING THROUGH AND BREAKING FORTH

Then I heard the Lord say, "In this season, I am releasing this mantle to bring about a restoration of the church to its true identity. In doing so, they will step into the breaker anointing. If they will be broken, I will cause them to break through and break forth."

I then had a vision of someone standing at a door. The Lord said, "This is a break through." This person stepped through the door, and it closed. Then I saw the same person break down the door and remove the door frame. The Lord said, "Break through is one-dimensional, breaking forth is generational."

I was reminded of Caleb—"But because My servant Caleb has a different spirit and follows Me wholeheartedly, I will bring him into the land he went to, and his descendants will inherit it."[1]

Caleb was of a different spirit. He was able to bring about generational possession of promise because he followed wholeheartedly. This is what the Father is looking for. Whole-hearted devotion. Verse 25 of Numbers 14 reveals a key for us—"Tomorrow turn."

The Lord is bringing about suddenlies where "tomorrow" there will be great possession of promises longing to be fulfilled.

THE IMPARTATION

I was then back in my living room with this angel standing in front of me. He handed me the mantle he was carrying. He said, "Release this mantle of the awakening, and as you do, watch the body be restored!"

So, I release this impartation of the mantle of awakening to you now! May you find yourself awakened to all that God has—walking in the fullness of the breaker anointing.

TEACHING MOMENT:
HINDRANCES TO BREAKTHROUGH

Hindrance One: Traditionalism!

"Jesus left there and came to His hometown [Nazareth]; and His disciples followed Him. When the Sabbath came, He began to teach in the synagogue, and many who listened to Him were astonished, saying, "Where did this man get these things [this knowledge and spiritual insight]? What is this wisdom [this confident understanding of the Scripture] that has been given to Him, and such miracles as these performed by His hands?"[2]

There are a lot of people who look at their tradition and say, "that's not how my church does it" or "that's not how I was taught."

JACOB BISWELL

If you treat your tradition as more sacred than the word of God, you will stop the flow of God on your behalf. Any kind of tradition that has its origins in a "works-mentality" can be a hindrance to receiving whatever it is that God has for you—this includes the law of the Old Covenant. Many people will reject anything that is contrary to the teachings of their denomination. I like to say, "God likes barbeque, and He has no issue roasting your religious cow!"

Traditions of men will shut down the healing and supernatural power of God in His church. We find that when Jesus entered Nazareth, He was unable to do many miracles. Tradition held them in their unbelief. In contrast, when Jesus entered Capernaum, those who were not hindered by tradition openly received the miracles of God.

Hindrance Two: Sin[3]

It is important to turn your back on sin—an unrepentant heart can hinder you from experiencing the Presence of the Lord. Sin is NOT always the hindrance to encountering the Lord, let me make that clear. Are you clean before the Lord? Sometimes people have a known sin in their lives that they refuse to deal with. We stand in the righteousness of Jesus—but that does not give us the license to sin. We must flee youthful lusts. If we are knowingly and willfully walking in disobedience, healing can be delayed or withheld altogether. When Jesus healed the blind man, He told him, "Go and sin no more lest a worse thing come upon you."[4] Sin hinders encountering the Lord and can cause an open door for the devil to attack you with sickness.

In my experience, the most common sin in the believer's life is

96

unforgiveness. If you are not in right standing with your brothers, it hinders the flow of the power of God. Jesus said that if you expect Him to forgive you, you must forgive others. Unity in the body of Christ is important for His supernatural power to flow.

Therefore, live righteously by walking in the spirit and not in the flesh.[5]

The Bible says in Psalm 84:11, "No good thing will He withhold from those who walk uprightly."

You want to know how to walk uprightly? Seek the Kingdom. That's the easiest way to stay out of sin. Seek the Kingdom, because when you're seeking the Kingdom, you're seeking Him. When your focus is on Him, you can't sin because you won't be distracted by the things that cause you to sin. It is possible to live a life where sin has no hold on you by seeking the Kingdom.

Hindrance Three: Lack of Faith or Unbelief![6]

Lack of faith is one of the biggest hindrances to the presence of the Lord. Faith is a major requirement to releasing the power of God on your behalf. Unbelief resists the power of God for your life. Many Christians are unbelieving believers. Even the disciples could not see miracles because of their lack of faith and Jesus even rebuked them for it.

Perhaps you basically believe the promises of God, but you have entertained the many doubts that are thrown into your mind either by society, by satan, or from other sources. If you don't stay diligently grounded in the word, doubt will begin to enter in.

It's very important that you're not wavering in faith,[7] but are "fully persuaded."[8] Some speak words of faith, but their actions contradict their words.[9] Some speak words of faith when they are around other faith walking people, but take them out of that environment and they lose all talk of faith. Their thoughts are no different. One moment they believe, and the next they are agreeing with thoughts of fear and unbelief. These people are double-minded. Scripture makes it clear that they will not receive anything from God.

Hindrance Four: Fear![10]

Worry and fear is the opposite of faith. It's faith in reverse—believing the wrong things. Worry and fear will produce ulcers and other health problems—it is working against you. There is no fear in faith. Perfect love will cast out all fear, and faith works by love. You cannot be in faith and fear at the same time. So, fear is another manifestation of unbelief.

Hindrance Five: Negative Confessions![11]

The words of your mouth reveal your faith. If you are walking in faith, it will show. It is critically important that we say about ourselves what God's word says about us. If God says we are healed, it is okay for us to say we are healed, regardless of how we feel. It's imperative that we consistently confess the Word. Our words give us direction, and He watches over His word to perform it on our behalf. We must continually speak His word over our situations.

Ultimately, no matter the hindrance, it pales in comparison to the authority Jesus has placed on the inside of you.

ENDNOTES

1. Numbers 14:24
2. Mark 6:1-2 (AMP)
3. Mark 6:12; 11:25; Pr.3:7-8
4. John 5:14
5. Romans 8:1-11
6. Mark 6:5-6; 9:23; Mt.14:31; 21:21
7. James.1:6-8
8. Romans 4
9. James 2
10. Matthew 6
11. Proverbs 6, 18; James 3; Isaiah 55:11

CHAPTER THIRTEEN

THE LEGITIMACY OF ENCOUNTERS

"And ye shall seek me, and find me, when ye shall search for me with all your heart." [1]

I have shared just some of the encounters that I have had over the last 19 years. I could write volumes about the times I have had with the Lord, and perhaps someday I will. I want to take the next couple of pages, however, to talk about the legitimacy of encountering the Lord. Many people have abused and misused the pulpit to bring glory to themselves. I want to try my best to help you create a basis of understanding for encounters. Obviously, this will take more than a few pages, so I hope that what I share will help you gain a better understanding of what it means to encounter God, by means of simply laying a foundation.

ENCOUNTERS

Throughout the centuries, there have been many people who have experienced trances, out-of-body experiences, and many other supernatural encounters. While some claim these experiences were from their spirit guides or chanting mantras, the ones that I want to focus on are those from the only pure and safe source of encounters…Christ Jesus.

It is important to remember that all encounters, trances, and other spiritual experiences must be in line with and according to scripture. There is an absolute danger when we begin to have encounters outside of the parameters of scripture. So, with that said, *all* encounters must be God-breathed. They must all be God-initiated. The word "encounter" implies something we didn't expect. The prophet Isaiah didn't go to the temple expecting to have a life-changing experience with the Lord, and yet, the Lord showed up. Out of it came one of my favorite passages where Isaiah describes the Lord being "high and lifted up."[2]

We cannot manipulate these experiences. We have only one responsibility, and that is to keep ourselves open to the Father. Many times, scripture says, "Let him who has an ear, hear what the spirit is saying."[3] We must have ears to hear, eyes to see, and a heart to receive. That way, when God does show up in some awesome way, we will be ready to listen.

The Bible says that God never changes; He still works and moves among his people in the same ways He did in the days of old. He moves in powerful and, many times, unexpected ways. The very sad reality is that many in the Body of Christ are content with a mundane and distant relationship with the Lord. They live from the idea that Jesus is off in a distant galaxy, and they are stuck here in this realm. This couldn't be further from the truth. He has chosen to take up residency within you. God *wants* to encounter you!

There are several encounters detailed throughout scripture that would blow our mind. 2 Corinthians 12:2-4 speaks of a man that Paul knew that was "caught up." Most scholars believe that Paul is speaking of himself here. Just a thought: were encounters so looked down upon that Paul was careful in even mentioning that he had one himself?

The Church has set such boundaries against this realm that it has become almost dangerous in some circles to even mention that God has spoken to you. There are even some groups that venture as far as to say that God is no longer speaking in any form other than the Bible. This is far from the truth, and I hope that in reading this book, you have uncovered the lies that you, yourself have believed about encountering God.

SOURCES AND SORCERY

There are many sources from which encounters come. They can be broken into four different categories:

1. God (Father, Jesus, Holy Spirit)
2. Satan or the demonic
3. Angels
4. Ourselves (Spirit, soul, flesh)

As we adventure into the realm of the spirit, it is very important to walk in a realm of discernment in order to decipher where our encounters are coming from. We must decide what we will receive and from where we will receive it. This can be very dangerous if we don't realize who or what is encountering us.

"For the word of God is quick, and powerful, and sharper than any two-edged sword, piercing even to the dividing asunder of soul and spirit, and of the joints and marrow, and is a discerner of the thoughts and intents of the heart."[4] Again, everything must line up with the word of God. We must ascertain the source of encounter and then make sure that we are in line with the word.

Another aspect in this journey of exploring the realm of the spirit is conjuring up our own desires. We must be careful in our approach to these things. If we begin to conjure them up on our own, we begin to operate in sorcery. It is very easy in our approach to encounters to get so caught up in our own desire that we forget the purpose of our pursuit of Him. We lose sight of where we are headed and end up encountering something we didn't plan on. Anything that doesn't bring forth fruit for the furthering of the gospel must be cut off.

THE ANGELIC

Many times, when I share my encounters with people, they get hung up on angels. While I don't have the ability to exhaustively cover the realm of the angelic, I do recommend Bobby Conner's book, *Heaven's Host—The Assignments of Angels Both Faithful and Fallen.* But I will cover just a few scriptures here that I have always referred to when talking about them. A lot happens in our daily lives that we are unaware of, and most of the time it has to do with angelic activity.

Throughout my life, I have had many encounters with angels. They have been a very real and strategic part of my life. I described the first angelic encounter that I remember earlier, but what I didn't mention is, that angel has never left my life. As I grew older, I began to see angels more often, even to the point where I would see them continuously.

Scripture speaks of these angels who are appointed by God to watch over us. The early church really understood this. There is a story in the book of Acts where Peter has been released from prison. He goes to Mary's house, and the servant girl, Rhoda, answers the door. She tells everyone that he is at the door, but they didn't believe her. They suggested it was his angel (Acts 12:15). So, the angelic played so much of a role in the early church, they thought it was his angel? It astonishes me that the church today barely even recognizes the fact that angels exist, let alone play a vital role in our lives!

Occasionally angels will come to give direction to people in unusually difficult circumstances. But they will not be female angels. Even at that, normal day-to-day guidance comes from the Holy Spirit within, not from angels.

"Let the peace which comes from Christ act as umpire continually in your hearts, deciding and settling with finality all questions that arise in your minds." (Colossians 3:15, Amplified)

"For as many as are led by the Spirit of God, they are the sons of God." (Romans 8:14)

The Bible is clear. Believers in Jesus Christ are to look to His Word and to the Holy Spirit within for guidance and not to angels.

Angels can cause circumstances to turn in your favor. They can deliver supernatural manifestations of love, comfort and deliverance. They can perform amazing feats of strength and operate in the supernatural. But they cannot teach and preach the Gospel and it is rare indeed that they bring guidance to the Believer. Not impossible, but rare.

Should an angel bring guidance to a believer, it will always be in line with the written word of God.

Angels are not "the Comforter" and they do not replace the ministry of the Holy Spirit, as some would have us to believe.

Still, some people believe that angels live on the inside of them and guide them from within. However, the Bible clearly reveals it is the Holy Spirit, not angels, who lives on the inside of you if you are a believer in Jesus Christ.

Others wrongly believe that when they die, they become angels. Angels are a separate entity, a separate creation, and are unrelated to man in every way other than that we all belong to the same family of God.

The angelic are important to the everyday life of the believer. Does that mean we worship them? Of course not! They can provide protection.[5] They can impart strength[6] and even provide food.[7] But we are never to worship them. Colossians 2:18 makes that clear: "Let no man beguile you of your reward in a voluntary humility and worshipping of angels..." Ask the Lord to show you how to work with the angelic, and don't worry, you'll know when they show up.

Here are some other scriptures for your study on the angelic:

- Hebrews 1:6-7, 14; 12:22
- Psalm 148:2-5, 68:17, 91:11-12, 104:4
- Matthew 26:53, 18:10, 4:11
- Luke2:13, 22:43, 1:11
- Job 38:7, 25:3

DELUSIONS OF GRANDEUR

I heard the Lord once say to me, "beware of delusions of grandeur." A **delusion of grandeur** is the false belief in one's own superiority, greatness, or intelligence. People experiencing delusions of grandeur do not just have high self-esteem; instead, they believe in their own greatness and importance even in the face of overwhelming evidence to the contrary.[8]

Many people place their ideas and greatness above the word of God. Understand my heart is not to debate or say anyone is wrong, but I do take issue with the statement that "not everything is in scripture." This is true to an extent. However, after the established word, everything must line up with it. The Bible is the word of God, and scripture will always confirm His voice.[9]

As far as confronting these "delusions of grandeur," it takes true Apostolic fathers to correct the messes being made across the body of Christ. "Open rebuke is better than secret love."[10] A lot of self-proclaimed prophets spew new-age doctrine, and people are gulping it up like it was straight from Jesus' mouth. The worst part of this is when they are questioned, they become very defensive. We as the body of Christ should not just take someone's word for it, but test all things.[11] On top of that, the Bible commands us to be discerning and judge the people in the Church.[12] Yes, I did say judge; there are a lot of people today who say, when you point out any error in leadership, "you are judging, and we as Christians are not supposed to judge, but act in love." That is a twisting of scripture that they try to hide behind because they don't want to have to have any accountability.

It is time for the Body of Christ to begin to execute "righteous judgment." We must come to the place where we allow accountability within our prophetic circles. Obviously, we are going to miss it at times, but I am not talking about "just missing it." The issue among most prophetic circles is that we just accept the word and don't judge it according to scripture. I define "righteous judgment" as Jesus did, "Not by mere appearances…"[13] If we take scripture out of context to say that "all judgement is forbidden" then we would forever prevent the church from walking in purity and holiness.

LINE IT UP

Our encounters must line up with the Word of God. The enemy will appear as an angel of light.[14] Anything that does not automatically bring God glory and serve as a purpose for the advancement of the Kingdom cannot be trusted. The lasting fruit of a true encounter with God is His peace and the kingdom expanded.

It doesn't matter how convincing they are, or how convinced the person himself is. Joseph Smith was convinced that God's angel met him to give him "another testament." We interpret our "extra-biblical" experiences in light of the revealed word of God.

There are other principles, too. For example, a lot of people say, "God told me to "_____ (fill in the blank)," and sometimes it's completely off. Does God speak to us? Of course. Does God speak to us things that are not in the Bible? Sure. However, God will never tell us to do something that contradicts what He has already written in His Word (for example, He won't tell you to do something He has already told you NOT to do).

The same goes with extra-biblical experiences. If someone says, "I went to heaven and saw _____", but what they say contradicts what the Bible has revealed about heaven, then we go with what the Bible says. Personal experiences should never be held in higher regard than the word of God. Everything should line up with scripture. God won't operate outside what he has established in His word. Anything outside of that is questionable.

The only cure for a delusion of grandeur is the release of real love, which contains discipline, correction, and truth.

WALK IN OBEDIENCE

Obedience is probably one of the most important, if not the most important, keys to accessing the kingdom. If you want the kingdom of God to come in and invade your life, obey the word of the Lord. Jesus lived His life obeying the Father.

One way Jesus demonstrated a life of obedience was through His sensitivity to the Father's leading when there was someone before Him who needed healing. There was not one person healed the same way. We see many instances of Jesus healing blind eyes, yet there is not one story that is alike. For one man, He spit in his eyes;[15] whereas in another instance, he spits on the dirt and makes mud, and then has the man wash in the pool of Siloam.[16] In still another example, Jesus declares healing through spoken word, and the man's eyes open.[17]

I can recall many times that I saw the kingdom manifested in my life because of obedience. One time, my wife and I were attending a Joan Hunter conference and the Lord spoke to me that we were to sow $1,000 into her ministry. Well, we didn't have $1,000 to give; in fact, we didn't have anything to give. The Lord told me, "I didn't ask you if you had $1,000." Therefore, we sowed $1,000 on credit. That's right, credit! I couldn't believe it myself (not that I am condoning this; you MUST have a word from the Lord for this kind of giving). What happened next blew us away. I can hardly summarize the numerous miracles of provision we saw released after this step of obedience.

Everywhere I went, people bought my groceries. I would pull into a restaurant, and they would give me my food for free. Pizza deliveries would come to my door; the delivery person would say they had an order for Pastor Jacob and give me a free pizza (exactly what I would have ordered in every instance). I would show up to the church, and bags of books and teachings would be waiting for me at the doorstep which, in and of itself was a miracle considering the location of our church and the neighborhood surrounding it. I would walk into a store where a giveaway was taking place for a gift card, and I would win it! One person sowed tens of thousands of dollars into us, which provided opportunities for personal needs to be met and gifts and offerings to be shared with others.

Not only did I see miraculous provision released for me and my wife, but the first time, I took my dog Charli with me to the church. I had brought an old pillow for her to lie on while I worked. Waiting for us at the door was a really nice dog mat and a $35 deer antler to keep her preoccupied. Did you catch that? Even my dog had favor!

All of what I shared above can be traced back to ONE simple step of obedience. I have had dreams in which the Lord gave me specific directions, and when followed, tremendous blessing would come upon me. It has been my experience that obedience produces harvest. However, planting seeds of obedience does not always produce immediate harvest. A simple look at nature, proves this point. We don't always see the harvest after planting the seed. Nevertheless, harvest will come in due season if we are faithful to the task at hand.

Sometimes responding with obedience to the voice and leadership of the Lord can pose a great struggle for our flesh. However, the Lord honors obedience. When Namaan was told to wash seven times in the Jordan River by Elisha's servant, he got offended and was going to turn away. Thankfully, he had persistent servants who urged him saying, "My father, if the prophet had told you to do some great thing, would you not have done it? How much more then, when he has said to you, 'Wash, and be clean?'"[18] So, in whatever God may ask you to do or to give, crucify your flesh (mind, will, and emotions), and be obedient. The Lord receives your offering of obedience and counts it to you as righteousness.

Obedience is what the Lord is asking for. There is no reward for those who live their lives repenting for disobedience. In 1 Samuel, we find the phrase "obedience is better than sacrifice," meaning it would be better to obey in the first place than have to repent for your disobedience. Just make the sacrifice and obey.

FINAL THOUGHTS

Anytime, you start talking about encounters, people seem to get caught up, and walls are put up. They say things like that is "new-age" or "super-spiritual." Well, I can respond with this: "We are in a *new age*—the kingdom age, when God is going to blow up our religious boxes." He is taking the church to a place it has never gone before. He is taking us beyond "normal Christianity" into a time where the supernatural is going to be key, and necessary for us to share the gospel. The truth is, the world isn't knocking down the door to get in our buildings anymore. They are looking for something real. They are looking for something that is beyond "religion."

In Dr. James Maloney's book *Establishing the Glory of the Godhead*, he writes, "We, following Christ's example, must cultivate an honor, and, indeed, a desire for the anointing—that is, to thicken it, as in the holy anointing oil is thickened – we must have a yearning for it (the anointing for the fruit, the anointing for the gifts) and covet its presence … As we honor His presence in our lives, He in turn entrusts to us the manifestations of His reputation to the people at large" (164).[19]

What he says is true; as we honor His presence, He entrusts us with more. The true sign of an encounter is that it points back to the Father. Everything we do or experience should bring glory back to Him, the one who simply *is*. He must be the source of the encounter. Anything else is fleshly at best, demonic at worst. We owe the world an encounter with God, but it starts with us encountering Him.

*I pray you will seek the Lord, encounter Him and in turn encounter the world! They are hungry for the truth, they are hungry for Him… **they just haven't realized it yet.***

ENDNOTES

1. Jeremiah 29:13

2. Isaiah 6

3. Matthew 11:15

4. Hebrews 4:12

5. Genesis 19:1, 11, 15; Daniel 6:22; Matthew 26:53; Acts 5:18,19

6. Daniel 10:8-11, 16-19; Matthew 4:11; Mark 1:13; Luke 22:43

7. 1 Kings 19:5-8

8. "Delusions of Grandeur." GoodTherapy.org. http://www.goodtherapy.org/blog/psychpedia/delusion-of-grandeur. Accessed 31 July 2017.

9. Matthew 24:35

10. Proverbs 27:5

11. 1 John 4:1

12. 1 Corinthians 5:11-13

13. Matthew 7:1-5

14. 2 Corinthians 11:14

15. Mark 8:23

16. John 9:6-7

17. Luke 18:42

18. 2 Kings 5:13 (AMP)

19. Maloney

THE FREE GIFT

Life without Jesus is truly meaningless, but life with Him becomes so much more! You can receive this life by believing with your heart and saying it with your mouth. Jesus is the only way to true peace. All you have to do if you want to know Him, is pray the following prayer:

Dear Lord Jesus, I know that I am a sinner, and I ask for Your forgiveness. I believe You died for my sins and rose from the dead. I turn from my sins and invite You to come into my heart and life. I want to trust and follow You as my Lord and Savior. In your name, Amen.

If you prayed that prayer, write to me at
www.equippingchurch.us
info@equippingchurch.us

I want to pray with you and help you find a good Bible-based, spirit-filled church to get plugged into! God bless you!

WORKS CITED

The Bible. Amplified Version, Zondervan, 2015.

The Bible. Authorized King James Version, Oxford UP, 1998.

The Bible. New Amerisan Standard Version, Lockman Foundation, 1995.

The Bible. New International Version, International Bible Society, 2011.

The Bible. New King James Version, Harper Collins, 1982.

"Delusions of Grandeur." GoodTherapy.org. http://www.goodtherapy.org/blog/psychpedia/delusion-of-grandeur. Accessed 31 July 2017.

Elwell, Walter A., Editor. *Baker's Evangelical Dictionary of Biblical Theology.* Grand Rapids, Michigan: Baker Books, 1996 USA.

"Emphanizō." *Smith's Bible Dictionary.* Barbour Publishing: 2012. *The KJV New Testament Greek Lexicon.* http://www.biblestudytools.com/lexicons/greek/kjv/emphanizo.html. Accessed 31 July 2017.

MEET THE AUTHOR

Jacob Biswell was born and raised in Dinuba, California. He jokes that while he wasn't born in Texas, he got there as soon as he could. He is passionate about people everywhere encountering the love of God.

He preached his first sermon at eight years old and was raised in the fires of Pentecost. He is madly in love with his wife Anna and their five children. They are the senior leaders of The Equipping Church in Bryan, Texas.

When Jacob is not spending time with his family or leading his church, he is the proverbial student. He holds two master's degrees: one in systematic theology and another in theology with a focus on cults and world religion. While his primary ministry focus is their local church, Jacob is available to speak at conferences, church services and ministry events from time to time.

www.equippingchurch.us

info@equippingchurch.us

Made in the USA
Coppell, TX
27 March 2022